Oxford
Botanic Garden
&
Arboretum

A BRIEF HISTORY

Oxford
Botanic Garden
&
Arboretum

A BRIEF HISTORY

Stephen A. Harris

Bodleian Library
UNIVERSITY OF OXFORD

IN ASSOCIATION WITH

University of Oxford Botanic Garden and Arboretum

First published in 2017 by the Bodleian Library
Broad Street, Oxford OX1 3BG

www.bodleianshop.co.uk

IN ASSOCIATION WITH
the University of Oxford Botanic Garden and Arboretum

ISBN: 978 1 85124 465 2

Text © Stephen A. Harris, 2017
Stephen A. Harris has asserted his right to be identified as the author of this Work

Images, unless specified on p. 144
© Bodleian Library, University of Oxford, 2017

Cover design by Dot Little at the Bodleian Library
Designed and typeset by Laura Parker in Trivia Humanist in 9pt on 13.3pt
Printed and bound by Prosperous Printing Co. Ltd., China, on 157gsm matt art (Neo FSC®) paper

MIX
Paper from
responsible sources
FSC® C001701

British Library Catalogue in Publishing Data
A CIP record of this publication is available from the British Library

Contents

Preface

the history and the manifold associations connected with the place, the long
line of professors and curators, the generations of scholars and statesmen,
of wits and divines, who have frequented this little enclosure, invest it with a
charm such as no other garden in the kingdom can lay claim

Anonymous, *Gardeners' Chronicle* (1885)

OXFORD BOTANIC GARDEN AND ARBORETUM is one of the world's oldest scientific plant collections, and, with a foundation date of 1621, the oldest surviving botanic garden in Britain. Conceived during a period of early seventeenth-century optimism as a place to grow medicinal plants, born in the turmoil of civil war and nurtured during the restoration of the monarchy, the Garden has, unsurprisingly, a curious past.

An organization as old as the Oxford Botanic Garden and Arboretum is like a biological organism; it evolves. Every generation the garden has adapted to its environment: an environment created by its physical location within a city; the social, scientific, economic conditions of the day; and the interests of the University and stewards of the garden. Each environmental change has left its mark. Parts of the organization are well adapted to current conditions, others appear redundant or superfluous – relics of previous adaptations.

This brief history of the garden, the first for over a century, aims to show how the garden's role in plant sciences in the University has varied with time. The garden was a botanical beacon in the late seventeenth century, only to be all but suffocated by the end of the eighteenth century, until the fire was reignited in the

FACING Daubeny's pool and fountain in the walled garden, looking north towards the Danby Gate.

The western and eastern conservatories, together with wood-and-glass, lean-to-type glasshouses either side of the Danby Gate, showing the 'Professor's House behind the Gate before it was knocked down to widen Magdalen Bridge. Metal engraving based on the *Oxford Almanack* (1766), as engraved by Joseph Skelton and published in 1820.

early nineteenth century. One feature has been consistent through the garden's history; the greatest successes have been when relationships among horticultural and academic staff are strongest. By tracing these relationships, this book aims to explain why the garden looks the way that it does.

The first five chapters of this history are arranged chronologically. They describe the garden's seventeenth-century origins, construction and planting, and the garden's subsequent evolution into the early twenty-first century, as ever more exotic plants were nurtured. The next four chapters are thematically arranged. One chapter looks at expansion of the garden to accommodate essential academic needs that support the living plants, for example, book and museum collections. A chapter on the arboretum shows how a new site, and a different soil, transformed the garden's planting environment. The garden's evolving rules, the efforts of staff to use the garden for teaching, and inspiring people outside the University, forms the basis of the next chapter. The penultimate chapter emphasizes an artificial fault line – descriptive versus experimental research – that has bedevilled much of the garden's twentieth-century history. The final chapter, which focuses on the physical separation of the garden and the Department of Plant Sciences in the 1950s, reflects on the consequences of this event.

There are echoes of the work started by the seventeenth-century stewards of the garden in today's activities. Social, political and intellectual conditions have changed dramatically over nearly four centuries, but plants remain fundamental to our existence. The garden's principles are the same: understanding plant diversity is essential if we are to improve our lives.

AUTHOR'S NOTE

UNTIL 1834, Oxford Botanic Garden was called the Physick or Physic Garden. For clarity, 'Botanic Garden' or 'Garden' will be used irrespective of the period under consideration. After 1963, the term 'Botanic Garden' or 'Garden' is understood to include the Arboretum. Quotations are as in original texts, except the long 's' has been converted to the modern 's' and ligatures have been split. Where necessary, clarifications have been added in square brackets. All prices are quoted from original documents. Questions frequently arise about equivalent values; hence conversions to 2015 equivalents have been given for guidance.[1] Common names are used in preference to scientific names in the main text; scientific equivalents may be found in Appendix A. Post titles, and lines of responsibility, change with time.[2] To avoid unnecessary confusion two general titles have been adopted in the main text; the person responsible for the practical work in the garden is the 'superintendent', whilst academic responsibility lies with the 'professor'. For more details of post holders, their dates and their titles, see Appendix B.

Builders of the University's botanical collections could never have conceived of the uses we make of their hard work. Therefore, my first thanks go to the centuries of unacknowledged individuals who have contributed to and looked after the botanical collections across the University, and made them the priceless resources they are today. I am grateful for access to manuscripts and photographs preserved in the Bodleian Library, the Botanic Garden and Arboretum, the British Library, Magdalen College, Oxford University Herbaria and the Royal Society. It is my sincere pleasure to thank many people (in alphabetical order) for their direct and indirect contributions to this history: John Baker, Anne Marie Catterall, Hugh Dickinson, Liam Dolan, Samuel Fanous, Simon Hiscock, Ben Jones, Barrie Juniper, Clare Kelly, Serena Marner, Richard Mayou, Valerie Parslow, Janet Phillips, Tom Price, Kate Pritchard, James Ritchie, Sophie Torrance, Jill Walker, Timothy Walker, Liz Woolley and Rosemary Wise and the members of the Oxford University and Harcourt Arboretum Florilegium Society. Of course, errors and misconceptions are mine, as are the views expressed. Finally, I thank Carolyn Proença for putting up with my fascination (perhaps obsession) with the past, present and future of University's botanical collections.

The herbaceous border and south wall.

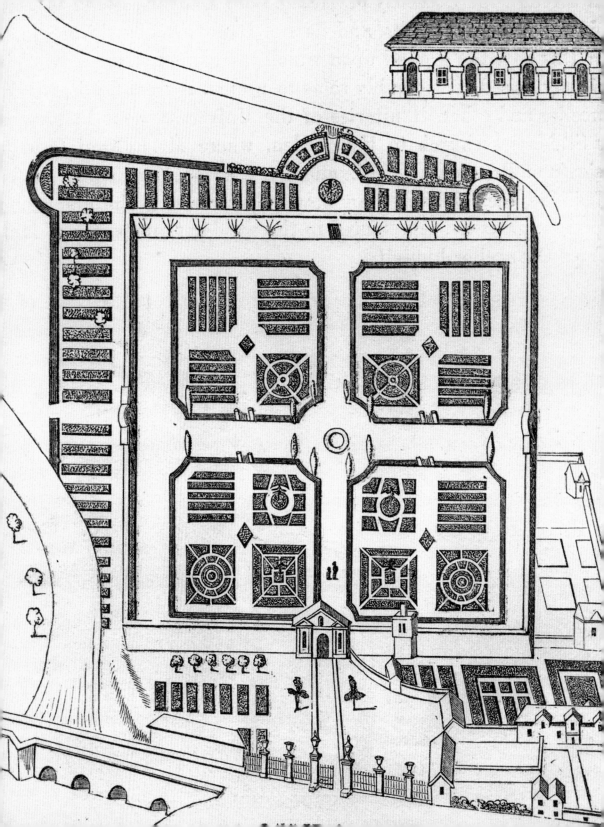

Founding the Garden

foreign pilgrimages, safety concerns and annoyances set aside

Preface to *Catalogus Plantarum Horti Medici Oxoniensis* (1648)

OXFORD GREW RAPIDLY IN SIZE, prosperity and influence during the sixteenth century. The city's appearance changed as grand buildings were erected to accommodate the expectations and pretensions of the expanding population. Furthermore, as the two powers in Oxford, the city ('town') and university ('gown'), vied for superiority, violent conflicts frequently broke out.[1] The University asserted that since it consisted 'of the flower of the nobility and gentry [it would] not endure to be subordinate to mechanical persons'.[2]

DESIRE FOR A GARDEN

At this time, science had yet to emerge as an independent discipline and plants were usually studied as part of medicine.[3] Across Europe medical training was changing. Physic gardens (collections of medicinal plants) were established, for example, at Pisa, Padua and Bologna in the 1540s, and at Leiden in the 1570s, but a petition to create one in Cambridge in the 1590s led to nothing.[4] By the seventeenth century, the medieval origins of Oxford's medical training had been reformed; it no longer relied on rote learning of classical texts but there was still little practical instruction, other than infrequent dissections of prisoners executed at Oxford Castle.[5] The absence of practical botanical instruction in medicine was nothing

FACING The 1675 Garden. Orlando Jewitt's wood engraving, based on David Loggan's map of East Oxford, published in Charles Daubeny's first guide to the Garden.

new. The Roman author Pliny had complained of medical students' attitudes to the plants they prescribed; it was 'more pleasant to sit in a lecture-room engaged in listening, than to go out into the wilds and search for the various plants'.[6]

Access to a garden might help students and their teachers recognize the plants they prescribed, and counter the supply of counterfeit medicines or the bulking out of expensive drugs with cheaper ones.[7] Furthermore, prescribing the wrong medicinal plants could be fatal, both to patients and their physicians' reputations. In 1620, in the University, 'motions were made for the founding of a ... Garden for Physical Simples'.[8] The atmosphere was right for establishing a physic garden.

To make the good intentions reality required largesse, innovation and commitment. Largesse came in the form of the bachelor-aristocrat Sir Henry Danvers. In a 'City of Palaces'[9] innovation was needed so Danvers' chosen site could be transformed into a garden to illuminate his reputation. Commitment came from the generations who worked in and for the Garden, often unsung, frequently in the face of indifference or hostility.

THE FOUNDER

Wiltshire-born, Oxford-educated Henry Danvers (1573–1644),[10] first Earl of Danby, was a soldier and landowner whose sober later years belied his bloody youth. In 1594, when he was 21 years old, Danvers and his elder brother, Charles (c.1568–1601),[11] killed a member of another prominent Wiltshire family;[12] it has been argued that the feud that was the backdrop to this event inspired Shakespeare's *Romeo and Juliet*.[13] The brothers fled to France, although four years later they were pardoned by Elizabeth I. Both brothers distinguished themselves in the military, their careers diverging soon after their return to England.

Charles was beheaded for conspiracy against the Queen. Henry established himself as a trusted courtier to King Charles I, whilst his younger brother John (c.1584–1655) developed a taste for horticulture and became one of the regicides who signed the king's death warrant in 1649.[14]

By the 1620s, despite the ignominy of his brother's execution, Henry Danvers had become a generous, very wealthy man.[15] Danvers' notion to create a garden in

FACING Henry Danvers, Earl of Danby. Detail from mezzotint by Valentine Green, published 1775, painted by Josiah Boydell based on van Dyck's portrait.

Oxford may have been inspired by the gardens he saw in exile, a desire to make a lasting mark ('for which no doubt he is in bliss'[16]), or perhaps, with the infirmity of his later years, self-interest. Unlike early Italian physic gardens, the Oxford garden was never the centre of a community of workshops occupied by the tradesmen of physic; herb collectors, processors and apothecaries.[17] If medicinal plants were ever supplied to the University's physicians, it was not a commercial operation.

In April 1621, Danvers gave the University £250 (c.£33,000 in 2015) to buy the lease of approximately five acres (c.2 hectares) of poorly drained, low-lying pasture on the west bank of the River Cherwell, opposite Magdalen College.[18] The land had been used as a burial ground for centuries, first by Oxford's Jewish community prior to their expulsion from England, and then by the Hospital of St John the Baptist, which stood on the site of Magdalen College until 1458.[19] Magdalen College became, and has remained, the Garden's landlord.

The 1620s and 1630s was a period of great expenditure for Danvers. Construction of the garden walls and gates cost him over £5,000 (c.£660,000 in 2015).[20] Major renovations were being made to his Oxfordshire home, Cornbury House,[21] and he had his portrait painted by the celebrated Flemish artist Anthony van Dyck (1599–1641).[22]

The Garden and its landlord, Magdalen College, in the 1930s.

TWO

Constructing the Garden

'Twas Gen'rous DANBY first enclos'd
The Waste, and in Parterres dispos'd;
Transform'd the Fashion of the Ground,
And Fenc'd it with a Rocky Mound

Evans, *Vertumnus* (1713)

A T T W O O'CLOCK, on Sunday 25 July 1621, the University's Vice-Chancellor, together with college and University members, processed, in their ceremonial finery, from the Church of St Mary the Virgin along the High Street to Danvers' leased plot. Following speeches by the University's senior members, a stone was laid; the Garden had been officially founded.[1]

GROUND AND WALLS

With the ceremonial complete, the hard, expensive work of creating a garden on an unpromising site began. Between 1621 and 1636 the level of the Garden was raised above the Cherwell. This was helped by Mr Windiat, the University's official scavenger, who was apparently responsible for ensuring streets, cess pits and middens were kept clean.[2] Windiat provided '4000 loads of mucke & dunge'[3]; immediate flooding was therefore averted but has remained a persistent risk to the Garden.

FACING Nineteenth-century view through the Danby Gate. Hand-coloured aquatint by Daniel Havell, based on a painting by Augustus Pugin, prepared for Rudolph Ackermann's *History of Oxford* (1814).

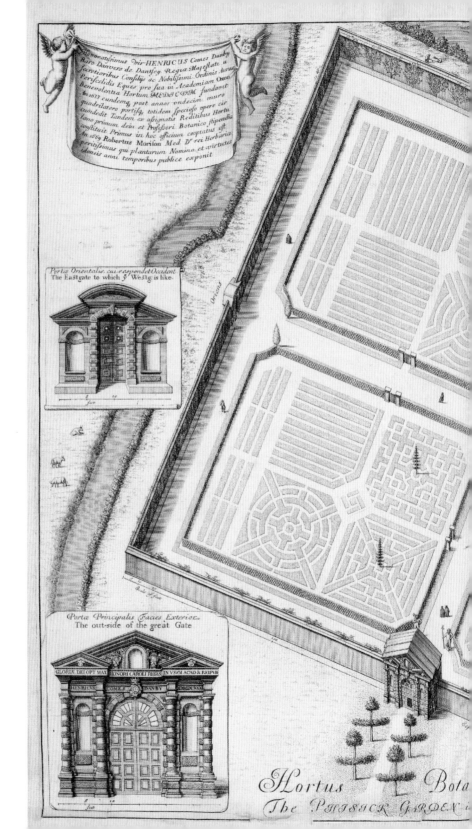

Portæ Orientalis, cui respondet Occident
The Eastgate to which ye Westg. is like.

Portæ Principalis Facies Exterior.
The out-side of the great Gate

GLORIÆ DEI OPT MAX HONORI CAROLI REGIS IN VSVM ACAD & REIPVB

HENRICVS COMES DANBY DD

Hortus Botanicus
The PHISICK GARDEN

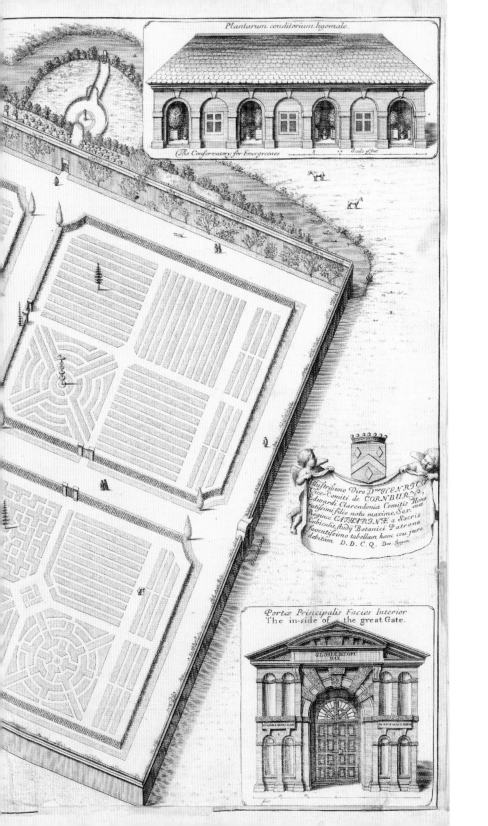

Plantarum conditorium hyemale.

The Conservatory for Evergreenes

Portæ Principalis Facies Interior
The in-side of the great Gate.

Illustrissimo Viro Dno HENRICO
Vice-Comiti de CORNBURY,
Edwardi Clarendoniæ Comitis Honoratissimi filio natu maximo, Ser. mæ
Reginæ CATHARINÆ a Sacris
Cubiculis, studij Botanici Patrono
faventissimo tabellam hanc ceu jure
debitam. D. D. C. Q. Dav. Loggan

Danvers' money bought a coping-topped, dressed stone wall with a rubble centre, 3–3.5 m high, up to 60 cm thick with a foundation more than 2.5 m deep. The wall, broken by three gates in the north, east and west walls, surrounds a piece of land approximately 103 m by 116 m.[4] The walls, 'well fair and sufficient as All Soules Colledge Walls, Magdalen Colledge Tower',[5] were completed in 1633, and made from local limestone, optimistically described as 'fit for all uses'[6] and extracted from quarries at Headington. When excavating the foundations for the wall and gates 'the bones of men, women and children were digged up'[7]; evidence of the land's former use. The walls were evidently completed from both ends; there is a poorly disguised join at the west end of the South Wall. Today, the Garden's walls and original gates are Grade I-listed buildings.[8]

The multipurpose garden wall marked territory and ownership, defining the Garden's limits and separating Danvers' gift from the rest of Oxford. The wall's grandiosity emphasized the University's prestige, at the same time protecting the enclosed area from unwelcome incursions. Besides physical protection, the wall had horticultural value as a windbreak and heat trap, helping tender plants grow and choice fruits ripen.[9]

GARDEN GATES

The original gates were built by Charles I's master mason Nicholas Stone (c.1586–1647), who also worked on Danby's Oxfordshire home.[10] The elaborate North (Danby) Gate, opposite Magdalen College, alone cost £500 (c.£62,000 in 2015);[11] it was completed in 1632. Features on the Gate's north face include the arms of Danvers, the University, St George and the House of Stuart. The niches on either side contain statues of Charles I and Charles II. The statues were added in 1693, and paid for by a fine levied against Oxford antiquarian Anthony à Wood (1632–1695) for libelling the University's Chancellor, Edward Hyde (1609–1674), First Earl of Clarendon.[12] Above the main entrance is a bust of Henry Danvers. The gate's inscription, 'Gloriae Dei Opt. Max. Honori Caroli Regis In Usum Acad. et Reipub. Henricus Comes Danby D.D. MDCXXXII', emphasizes the glory of God and Charles I, the utility of the Garden for the University and Britain and immortalizes the

PREVIOUS PAGE Layout of the Garden in 1675, showing quartering by yew hedges and the 'Conservatory for Evergreenes' in the top right corner. Copper engraving by David Loggan.

The East Gate from outside the walled garden.

Bookplate used in the Garden Library from c.1790. The plate was replaced
in the nineteenth century by a much-inferior version, lacking the 'J'.

name of Henry Danvers. The Danby Gate was originally closed by a huge, wooden, two-leaved panelled door.[13] Today, a pair of iron gates, made from railings that surrounded St Frideswide's tomb in Christ Church Cathedral, serves this purpose.[14] The East Gate, towards the river, and West Gate, towards the city centre, are similar in design. Originally, both gates were closed by two-leaved panelled doors, a feature seen only on the West Gate today.

Three gates proved too few, so walls were knocked through and corners knocked out as the Garden tried to break the confines of its birth. Soon after the original gates were finished, a small gate was driven through the centre of the South Wall, which, by the 1730s, had become the opening seen today, except barred by an iron gate.[15] Another gate was added to the east end of the South Wall, probably in the eighteenth century. Two small gates were added to the North Wall on either side of Danby Gate during the eighteenth century. The eastern one is today the Garden's public entrance; the western one was lost during major redevelopments of the

Drawn & Engraved

by J. Whessell, Oxford.

VIEW FROM THE PHYSIC GARDENS.

View from the Garden through the Danby Gate, with the Bobarts' north–south yew hedges in the foreground.
Copper engraving by John Whessell for the title page of his *Oxford delineated* (1831).

North Wall in the late nineteenth century.[16] A small tower appears in an early image of the North Wall but is absent in subsequent images.[17]

The north-east corner of the wall was probably demolished in the eighteenth century. Today, only the wall's south-west corner is intact.

OXFORD LANDMARK

Inside the walled garden, glimpsed through the Danby Gate, is a classic Oxford view. In the seventeenth century this view was only possible when the wooden doors were open. By the 1730s, a great circle, above eye level, had been cut in the gate, although the gates were solid once again by 1766.[18] The solid doors give the impression of exclusion and exclusivity. The iron gates made their appearance in the mid-nineteenth century, although the view from the south had been public since the early eighteenth century.[19] By the late nineteenth century the Danby Gate was covered in ivy. Despite such romanticism, at least one nineteenth-century writer regarded a North Wall entrance as detrimental to the Garden; the ivy was removed in 1900.[20] The Danby Gate, throughout the centuries, has symbolized the Garden. It appears on book plates, stationery and library stamps from the late eighteenth century and was used by the University's Department of Plant Sciences until the early twenty-first century. As a symbol, the Danby Gate has now lost its appeal, but changes of fortune are nothing new. In 1649, when Charles I was executed, the Gate's strong royal associations made it a target for vandals; eleven years later, when the throne was restored, repairs cost the Garden £1 1s (c.£110 in 2015).[21] The royal statues eventually lost their arms, and smoke from college and city buildings left its marks on Stone's work.[22]

Porcelain plate showing Jacob Bobart the Elder in front of the Danby Gate,
c.1755. Based on the frontispiece to Abel Evans' poem *Vertumnus* (1713).

THREE

Planting the Garden

At His Command the Plat was chose,
And Eden from the Chaos rose:
Confusion in a Moment fled,
And Roses blush'd where Thistles bred.

Evans, *Vertumnus* (1713)

In 1642, approximately two decades after the foundation stone was laid, Jacob Bobart the Elder (*c.*1599–1680) was made the Garden's first superintendent. As Bobart took up his post, English politics was changing dramatically; Parliamentarians were routing Royalists from power in the English Civil War and the king fled to Oxford.[1] Despite the inconvenience, the University continued its business very much as usual, just as it would once the monarchy was restored.[2] In mid-seventeenth-century England, cultivation of a garden was considered by some as part of a righteous life, whilst market gardens were needed to feed Oxford's population.[3] Furthermore, men who would later form the Royal Society started questioning preconceived ideas about the natural world. Bobart found himself among a community of city and college gardeners who probably exchanged techniques, observations, seeds and cuttings,[4] and was able to take advantage of a heady mix of mystical, practical and experimental interest in plants. Then, as now, visitors expected to find exotic plants in a botanic garden, and the Bobarts developed conservatories and stovehouses (precursors to glasshouses) in order to cultivate these tender specimens.

BOBART THE ELDER

Jacob Bobart the Elder appears to have been in the right place at the right time. In 1637, Danvers approached the high-profile gardener to Charles I, John Tradescant the Elder, and 'came to some reasonable good terms' with him to become superintendent.[5] However, Tradescant died the following year and there is no evidence he ever took up the post.

We know little of Bobart, the 'Germane Prince of Plants',[6] other than he was a tall, strong, Brunswick-born, former soldier and an eccentric publican of integrity with a penchant for topiary.[7] Contemporary portraits show a long-bearded, rather severe-looking man who might 'hold his own among the dons of the University', and who was the butt of town-and-gown wits.[8] Bobart married twice, had at least ten children, of which his eldest son (Jacob) became his successor.[9] He was a wealthy, literate man who, when he died, had leases for the profitable 'Greyhound Inn and meadow' (east corner of Longwall Street and High Street[10]) and houses at Smythgate (north Catte Street), owned a house on George Lane (George Street) and bequeathed more than £115 (c.£13,000 in 2015) to his daughters and divided his library between his sons Jacob (1641–1719) and Tilleman (1662–1724).[11] Despite running the Garden, neither he nor his son was ever a member of the University.

Danvers offered Bobart a lease on the Garden site subject to his good behaviour and appropriate care for the Garden; his annual salary was £40 (c.£4,700 in 2015) and the income from the Garden's produce.[12] Bobart made a healthy living from his commercial interests in the city and from the Garden for decades.[13] Bobart's concentration on productivity appears to have affected the Garden; in 1664, during his English tour, the curmudgeonly French physician Samuel de Sorbiére (1615–1670) dismissed the Garden as 'small, ill kept, and more like an Orchard than a Garden'.[14] Five years later, Cosimo III de' Medici (1642–1723), Grand Duke of Tuscany thought the Garden 'scarcely deserves to be seen' from the 'smallness of its site, irregularity, and bad cultivation', although he admired Bobart the Elder.[15] However, the University evidently thought the Garden a jewel as distinguished visitors, such as the Prince of Orange (future King William III; 1650–1702), were paraded through it,[16] and gentlemen, such as John Evelyn (1620–1706) and Elias Ashmole (1617–1692), had nothing but praise for the Garden and Bobart's work.[17]

FACING Jacob Bobart the Elder, the first Keeper of the Garden, who set the Garden's appearance for more than a century. Oil painting.

For over a decade (1669–1683), Jacob Bobart the Elder's horticultural successes were complemented by the appointment of the first Professor of Botany in a British university, the Royalist Civil War veteran, and physician to Charles II, Robert Morison (1620–1683).[18] Morison taught in the Garden, whilst Bobart started to build a herbarium and library. Bobart and Morison proved to be the first great Garden partnerships, providing the Garden with firm horticultural and academic foundations. Such a partnership did not emerge again until the 1830s.

BOBART THE YOUNGER

Oxford-born Bobart the Younger remained at the Garden his whole career.[19] First, he worked for his father, then as superintendent in his own right when his father died. Bobart maintained his father's practice of selling plants, acting as a rare-plants nurseryman for wealthy gardeners; whether raising money for the Garden or himself is unclear.[20] The younger Bobart was widely travelled and highly respected by scholars and gardeners in Britain and Europe. He was also a practical joker; he created a serpent in his metaphorical Eden by (in)famously fashioning a rat's corpse into a dragon.[21] When Morison was killed in 1683, Bobart took on his teaching and academic duties, but not the professorial title.[22] During the 1680s, Bobart fostered a life-long friendship with the English diplomat William Sherard (1659–1728).[23] Bobart was crucial in developing Sherard's botanical interests and enthusiasm for herbaria (dried plant collections); Sherard eventually amassed 'the most ample, authentic, and valuable botanical record in the world',[24] which he bequeathed to the University in 1728. Two years before he died, illness forced Bobart briefly to leave the Garden in the care of his half-brother, Tilleman Bobart.[25] Tilleman exceeded the Garden's budget, and Jacob was forced to resign. He was allowed to remain in his home, although months before Bobart's death Sherard had complained, 'they [the University] ought to have let him spend the short remainder of his time in the Garden'.[26]

Physically, Bobart the Younger was a 'shrimp' compared with his father.[27] One visitor thought his appearance accorded with neither his horticultural nor academic reputation: 'an unusually pointed and very long nose, small eyes deeply set in his head, a wry mouth with scarcely any upper lip, a large and deep scar on one cheek, and his whole face and hands as black and coarse as those of the meanest gardener or labourer'.[28]

Jacob Bobart the Younger, the second Keeper of the Garden. Oil painting.

William Sherard, founder of the Sherardian Chair and major benefactor
to the Garden and University Herbaria. Oil painting.

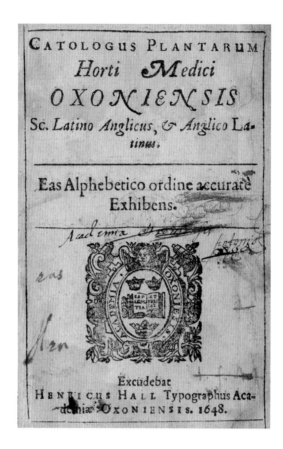

THE BOBARTS' PLANTS

Bobart the Elder is credited with authorship of the anonymous *Catalogus plantarum horti medici Oxoniensis* (1648), the first catalogue of the Garden's plants; the 1,369 plants mentioned are identified by Latin phrase names and common names.[29] A decade later a more detailed catalogue, written by two Oxford academics helped by the Bobarts, contained 1,889 names.[30] In 1676 Bobart the Younger compiled a 1,113-name list of the Garden's plants; this appears to have been the last time a complete inventory of the Garden's plants was made until the 1990s.[31]

Placing modern scientific names on the Bobarts' plant names is a major academic challenge, which would be impossible if they had not carefully preserved

26

The South Gate and pool in the Lower Garden in winter, looking north towards the Danby Gate (January 1867). Bobart's yews, planted c.1645, are behind the pillars, the left-hand one has survived to the present day. Photograph taken by Douglas William Fairchild.

FACING Title page of the Garden's first catalogue published in 1648, from a copy in William Sherard's personal library.

samples of pressed dried plants (herbarium specimens).[32] In the Bobarts' time, such collections were unusual, expensive objects. In his poem praising Bobart the Younger, Abel Evans (1675–1737) paid particular attention to the herbarium:

> *Thy* Hortus Siccus [herbarium] *still receives:*
> *In Tomes twice Ten, that Work immense!*
> *By Thee compil'd at vast Expence;*
> *With utmost Diligence amass'd,*
> *And shall as many Ages last.*[33]

On 5 November 1665, Samuel Pepys (1633–1703) described his surprise at the novelty of being shown John Evelyn's herbarium: 'leaves laid up in a book of several plants kept dry, which preserve colour, however, and look very finely, better than any Herball'.[34] The Bobarts' herbaria are the founding collections of Oxford University Herbaria, which today contains more than one million specimens; it is one of the world's great plant collections.[35]

Comparing the names in the Bobarts' catalogues with those on the herbarium specimens it is possible to give modern names to the species they grew. The lists show that nearly 2,570 names were used by the Bobarts, of which more than 530 were common to all lists. Species that have been continually grown in the garden include the Garden's oldest tree, a yew apparently planted by Bobart the Elder in 1645, the sole living link the Garden has with its founding superintendent. In the Bobarts' time this evergreen tree was planted for its aesthetic, rather than medicinal properties.[36]

Indeed, the Bobarts' Garden was much more than a collection of plants with apparent medicinal properties. Medicinal plants, such as mandrake[37] and rosemary,[38] comprise fewer than 20 per cent of the plants grown. Other plants included introductions from the Americas such as tobacco[39] and the American agave,[40] whilst variegated plants, collected from the wild and college gardens, were a speciality.[41] Horticultural favourites included numerous morphological and colour forms of anemones, oriental hyacinths and wallflowers. Furthermore, Bobart the Elder was a well-known auricula breeder.[42] The Bobarts also grew curiosities such as the surprising 'humble plant', whose leaves folded when touched.[43]

FACING Forms of hollyhocks growing in the Garden in the late seventeenth century. Dried plant specimens annotated by Bobart the Younger.

Malva rosea folio subrotundo flore pleno.
C.B.P. Diversorum colorum.

b Morison

Alcea Ricini fol. Virgin. flo. albo
parvo Br. pr. 2. Althea Ricini
fol. Virgin. H.L.B.

M. A. H. I. 524. N. 20

Humble plant. The leaves fold when touched and intrigued
Garden visitors in the late seventeenth century.

Portrait of medlar, a fruit commonly consumed during the Bobarts' time. Watercolour
by botanical artist Rosemary Wise, co-founder of the Oxford University Botanic Garden
and Harcourt Arboretum Florilegium Society.

The cultivation of novelties drew competition. In 1699, an unidentified correspondent sent Bobart the Younger a few leaves of the 'humble plant', adding 'this is to show Mr Bobart how well my plants keep'.[44]

By the end of the seventeenth century the walls of the Bobart's Garden were covered with trained trees and shrubs that probably included at least 15 types of cherries, three types of almonds, two types of medlar, apricot and quince, and 'divers kindes' of peaches, pears, apples, and black and white plums.[45] Double pomegranates, to the height of the walls, covered with 500 flowers, grew and, in 1661, ripe figs were presented to the University's Chancellor.[46] In 1670, the Bobarts had a purpose-built, tiny-windowed conservatory outside the Garden's North Wall; 'to preserve tender plants & trees from the Injury of hard winter'.[47] They grew seven sorts of myrtle and five sorts of citrus, together with many other tender plants.[48] By 1733, a storey had been added to the building and it had become the professor's house, library and herbarium.

The seeds and plants that stocked the Bobarts' Garden came from their own collections made in the wild, gifts from friends and colleagues and exchange with fellow gardeners; some plants may even have been purchased. A premium was attached to maximizing the numbers of species in the collection.

FACING Jacob Bobart the Elder in front of the Danby Gate with a goat and dog. On high days and holy days Bobart tagged his beard with silver, whilst the yews clipped in the form of giants inspired ballads in the 1660s. Copper engraving that is the frontispiece of Abel Evans' *Vertumnus* (1713), a poem praising Jacob Bobart the Younger. The pelican over the gate traditionally symbolizes a son's respect for his father.

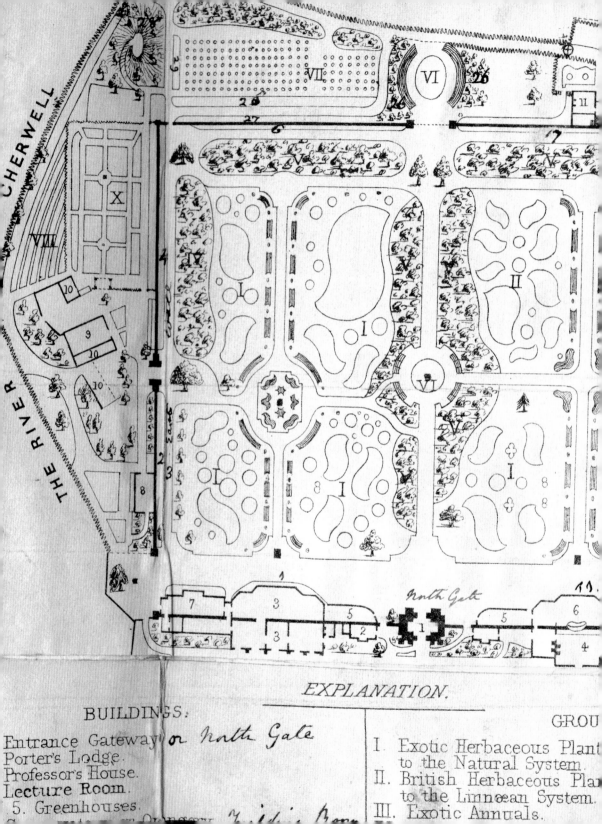

CHERWELL

THE RIVER

North Gate

North Gate

EXPLANATION.

BUILDINGS:

Entrance Gateway or North Gate
Porter's Lodge.
Professor's House.
Lecture Room.
5. Greenhouses.

GROU

I. Exotic Herbaceous Plant
to the Natural System.

II. British Herbaceous Plant
to the Linnæan System.

III. Exotic Annuals.

FOUR

Evolution

Academic Gardens tho' greatly inferior in Magnificence &
Splendour to those supported by Royal Expenditure may be
considered as the more useful Schools of Botany

Sibthorp, *Lecture notes (c.1788)*[1]

THE GARDEN'S HEART is the walled garden. When the 33-year-old English lady Celia Fiennes (1662–1741) visited Oxford in 1694 she claimed the 'variety of flowers and plants [in the Garden] would have entertained one a week'.[2] The Garden Miss Fiennes saw was quartered by two broad, tree-studded paths running north–south and east–west.[3] Each quarter was protected by a yew hedge and two metal, presumably bolted, gates. Within each quarter, numerous small beds were arranged in formal, geometric patterns. Despite images and our knowledge of the Garden's plants we have few ideas of how the plants were arranged. Perhaps they were laid out according to medicinal or other utilitarian use, or geographically, the world divided into four continents, emphasizing the Garden as a representation of Eden.[4] Images of the Garden during the Commonwealth show a quartered Garden but the Restoration formality may have been Morison's influence, following his experiences at Gaston (1608–1660), Duke of Orléans' garden during his exile.[5]

The walled garden was only a portion of the Bobart's Garden; a ditch beyond the South Wall marked the end of their domain. The ditch was apparently clay-lined and planted with bog plants, and clustered around a hastily constructed South Gate were formal borders and an area for potted plants.[6] The South Gate was also a convenient entrance to the Garden from across Christ Church Meadow.

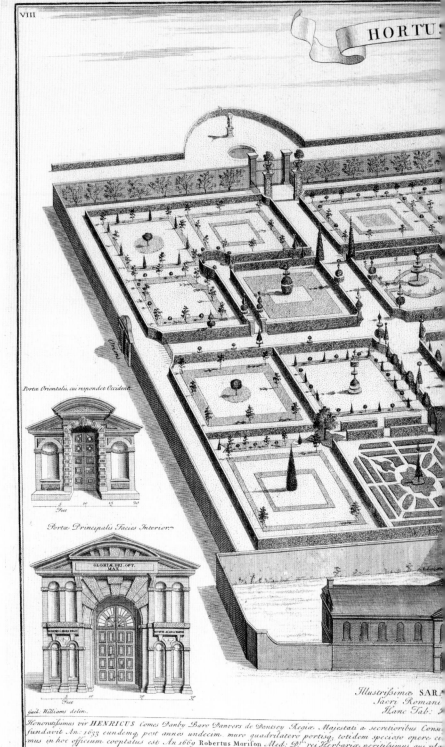

HORTU

Portæ Orientalis, cui respondet Occidens.

Portæ Principalis Facies Interior.

GLORIÆ DEI OPT. MAX.

Guil. Williams delin.

Illustrissimæ SARA
Sacri Romani
Hanc Tab:

Honoratissimus vir HENRICUS Comes Danby Baro Danvers de Dantsey Regiæ Majestati a secretioribus Consi
fundavit An: 1633 eundemq, post annos undecim muro quadrilatero portisq, totidem specioso opere c
mus in hoc officium cooptatus est An 1669 Robertus Morison Med: Dr rei Herbariæ peritissimus qui pla

Plantarum conditorium hyemale.

Septentrio

GLORIÆ DEI OPT MAX HONORI CAROLI REGIS IN VSVM ACAD.& REIPVB.

HENRICVS   COMES   DANBY DⁿMDCXXXII

Porta Principalis Facies Exterior.

5   10   Pedes   20   30

MARLBOROUGH

cipissæ &c.

Cail: Williams.

ni, Ordinis Aureæ Periscelidis Eques pro sua in Academiam Oxon Benevolentia, Hortum MEDICUM
dem ex assignatis Reditibus Hortulano primum, dein et Professori Botanico stipendia constituit Pri
x et virtutes idoneis anni temporibus publice exposuit.

Fellow of Magdalen, Joseph Addison (1672–1719), a contemporary of Bobart the Younger, preferred 'natural' over manicured landscapes and commented: 'we see the marks of the scissors upon every plant and bush'.[7] By the 1730s, the Garden's formality had become more extreme, but as the century dragged on the Garden's formality declined, and under Humphrey Sibthorp's (c.1713–1797) stewardship, any naturalism was probably the result of indifference rather than planning.[8] His successor, his son John (1758–1796),[9] re-established order by grubbing up the double row of yew hedges along the east–west path, redesigning the beds and planting on a broadly geographical basis: Britain and Europe east of the north–south path, North America and Asia to the west. Sibthorp's plants showed 'their Natural Growth, neither disguised nor distorted by Art'; their detailed arrangement reflecting his teaching interests.[10]

Garden rearrangements, together with developments in the city, saw professorial homes expanded, demolished and rebuilt, before being demolished again. Humphrey Sibthorp had his home (now part of St Hilda's College) built in Cowley Place, which provided a pleasant, conveniently distant, view of the Garden; although it apparently ruined the Dean of Christ Church's view.[11] Superintendents of the Garden have generally lived on site. Bobart the Elder apparently used the Greyhound Inn, opposite the Garden, whilst in the eighteenth century a tied cottage was built just south of the Garden's south-west corner for the gardener.[12]

CONSERVATORIES AND GLASSHOUSES

Visitors expect exotic plants in botanic gardens. Yet satisfying this expectation is onerous, as keepers of the Garden have repeatedly discovered. In 1737, one year after visiting Oxford, the Swedish botanist Carolus Linnaeus (1707–1778) bemoaned his lot:

> to strike ones head against the limits of the world, to view the sun, where it never sets, this is not for the life of a single Botanist, or for his purse ... The Botanist requires world wide commerce, libraries of practically all books published about plants, gardens, greenhouses, hothouses, and gardeners.[13]

PREVIOUS PAGE The Garden as etched by William Williams in his *Oxonia Depicta sive Collegiorum et Aularum in Ipclyta Academia Oxoniensi Ichnographica & Scenographi* (1733).

The walled garden in 1822, looking north-east towards the Danby Gate with the western conservatory visible. Despite the garden's rules, women and a child are visiting, whilst a young gardener turns soil. The north–south yew hedge is clearly visible on the right.
Metal engraving by James Sargant Storer and his father Henry.

In short, as with hardy cultivation, exotic plants needs skill and time but above all – money – to flourish. For centuries, gardeners have used all manner of ruses to improve the protection provided to their exotic charges.

Glasshouses, the nineteenth-century temples to exotic horticulture, were not sudden innovations; they evolved from seventeenth-century heated stovehouses via fruit walls and unheated conservatories (orangeries).[14] Bringing plants indoors for the winter protects expensive exotics but there were cheaper protective tricks, such as pits, matting and bell jars.[15]

If gardeners get conditions right, exotic plants grow actively. Vast improvements in the quality and range of plants grown under protection were made as tropical latitudes were explored during the seventeenth and eighteenth centuries, the science of plant propagation improved, refinements were made in heating and glass technologies and gardeners gained experience.[16] Unsurprisingly, a powerful driver was one-upmanship.

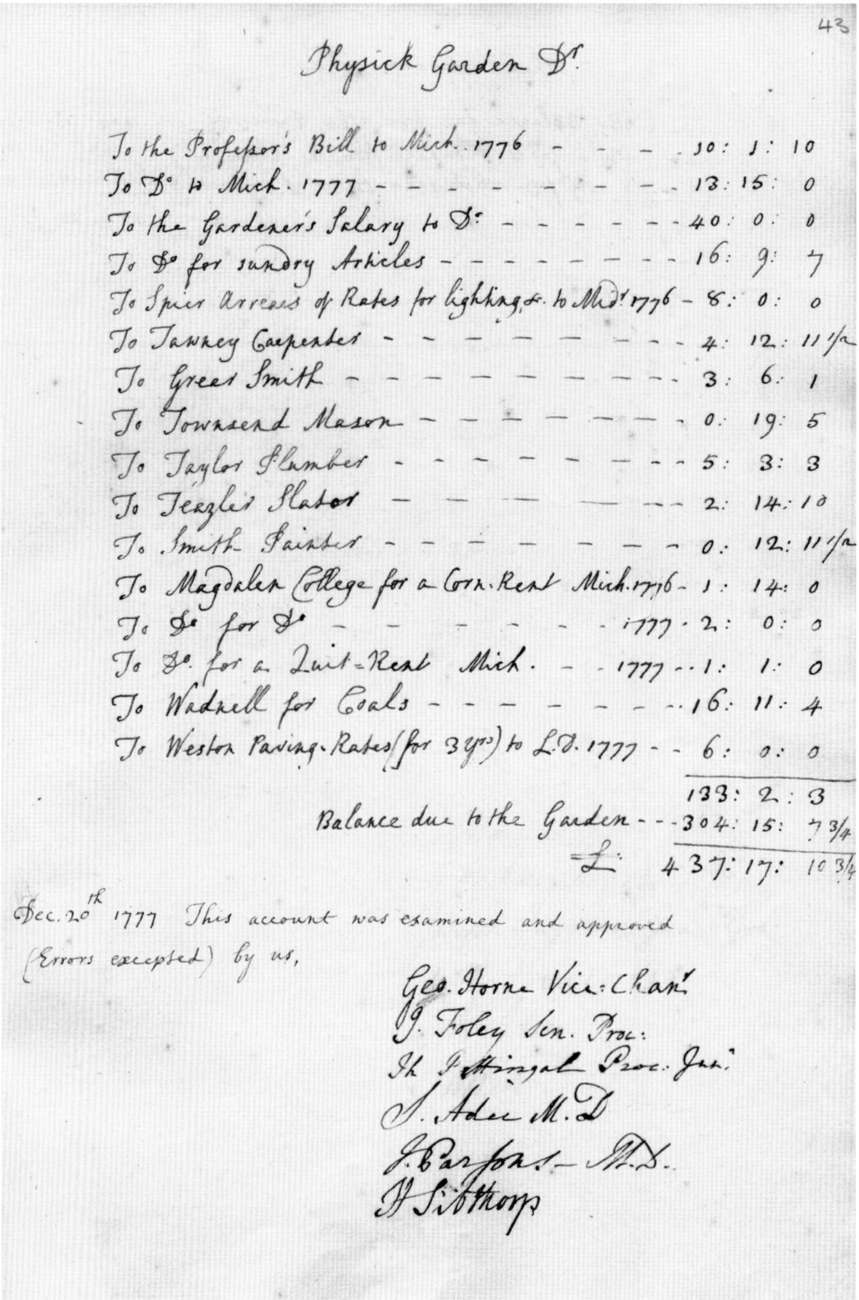

Physick Garden Dr.

	£	s	d
To the Professor's Bill to Mich. 1776 — — — —	30	1	10
To Do to Mich. 1777 — — — — — — —	13	15	0
To the Gardener's Salary to Do — — — — —	40	0	0
To Do for sundry Articles — — — — — — —	16	9	7
To Spier Arrears of Rates for lighting &c. to Mid.t 1776 —	8	0	0
To Tawney Carpenter — — — — — — — —	4	12	11½
To Great Smith — — — — — — — — —	3	6	1
To Townsend Mason — — — — — — —	0	19	5
To Taylor Plumber — — — — — — —	5	3	3
To Teagles Slator — — — — — — —	2	14	10
To Smith Painter — — — — — — — —	0	12	11½
To Magdalen College for a Corn Rent Mich.1776 —	1	14	0
To Do for Do — — — — — — 1777	2	0	0
To Do for a Quit Rent Mich. — 1777	1	1	0
To Wadnell for Coals — — — — — —	16	11	4
To Weston Paving Rates (for 3 yrs) to L.D. 1777 —	6	0	0
	133	2	3
Balance due to the Garden — —	304	15	7¾
£	437	17	10¾

Dec. 20th 1777 This account was examined and approved
(Errors excepted) by us,

Geo. Horne Vice.Chanr

I. Foley Sen. Proc:

Th Pettingal Proc. Jun:

S. Adee M.D

J. Parsons M.D.

H. Sibthorp

Garden accounts for 1776–1777 showing gardener's salary, rent and heating costs.
Among the people signing the accounts are the University's Vice-Chancellor and Humphrey Sibthorp.

'A heating apparatus of the olden time' that was still used in the
Garden glasshouses in the mid-nineteenth century. Woodcut.

This was a race a poorly funded university garden was unwise to join, as
John Sibthorp told his students in the late 1780s: 'a garden which has no Fund
for its Increase can Support a very feeble Contest with those fostered by Royal
Munificence or even those on which private Fortunes are lavished'.[17] Nevertheless,
from the early eighteenth century onwards, the Garden did become involved.

Manipulation of the indoor environment was hit-and-miss but light levels, air
quality and temperatures were important. By the late seventeenth century, the
English diarist John Evelyn was using the newly invented thermometer in practical
gardening; five decades later it symbolized the gardener's mastery over nature.[18]
Traditionally, glasshouses were directly heated through open fireplaces and iron
stoves.[19] One Victorian commentator was horrified at the primitive technology the
Garden was using in its conservatories well into the nineteenth century: 'it will
scarcely be credited that this apparatus [an iron trolley loaded with smouldering
coals hauled around by a gardener] was in use in the old conservatory ... within
the memory of the present Curator [William Hart Baxter]. Hot-water pipes were
not then in use, and flues were not existent even so late as fifty years ago [c.1835]'.[20]
By comparison, the Chelsea Physic Garden's conservatories and glasshouses had
benefited from indirect heating since 1684.[21] Crude, direct heating, such as the
Oxford trolley, was essentially uncontrolled, and the atmosphere became polluted,
creating noxious conditions for plants and gardeners alike. Chelsea's indirect
heating was comparatively controllable and clean. Despite the Garden's primitive
heating technology, the Bobarts were acclaimed for their sensitive plants and, in
the eighteenth century, the Garden became home to a collection of succulents
'long boasted a pre[-]eminence over the other Gardens of Europe'.[22]

In the early eighteenth century, if the Garden was to maintain its horticultural
reputation it needed to invest in appropriate technology. But the cost of glasshouses

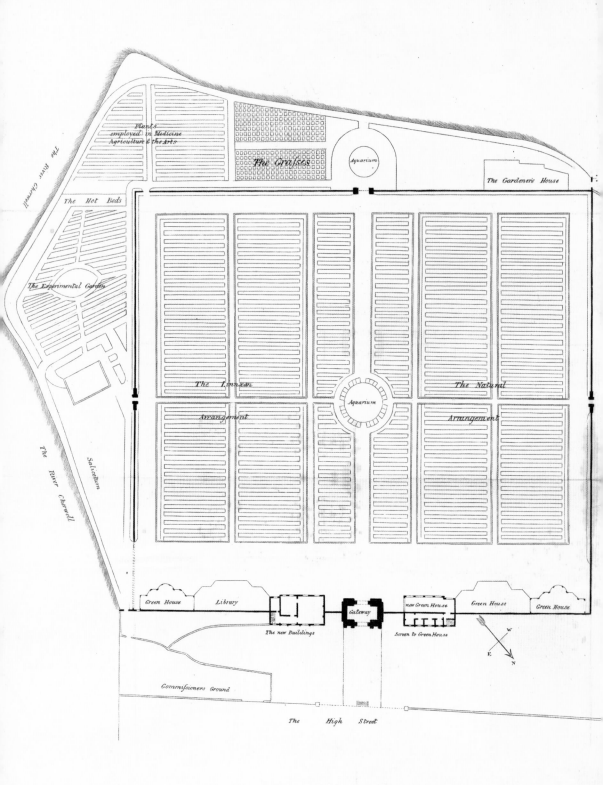

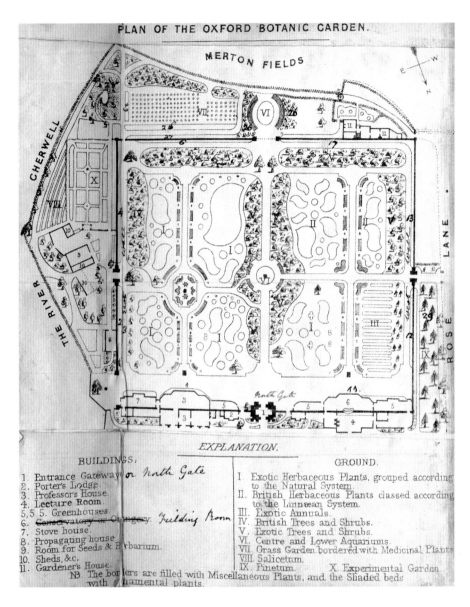

PLAN OF THE OXFORD BOTANIC GARDEN.

MERTON FIELDS

CHERWELL

THE RIVER

ROSE LANE

North Gate

EXPLANATION.

BUILDINGS.

1. Entrance Gateway or North Gate
2. Porter's Lodge.
3. Professor's House.
4. Lecture Room.
5,5 5. Greenhouses.
6. Conservatory or Orangery. Fielding Room
7. Stove house.
8. Propagating house.
9. Room for Seeds & Herbarium.
10. Sheds, &c.
11. Gardener's House.

GROUND.

I. Exotic Herbaceous Plants, grouped according to the Natural System.
II. British Herbaceous Plants classed according to the Linnæan System.
III. Exotic Annuals.
IV. British Trees and Shrubs.
V. Exotic Trees and Shrubs.
VI. Centre and Lower Aquariums.
VII. Grass Garden bordered with Medicinal Plants
VIII. Salicetum.
IX. Pinetum.   X. Experimental Garden

NB. The borders are filled with Miscellaneous Plants, and the Shaded beds with Ornamental plants.

Layout of Daubeny's Garden in 1850, with annotations by Charles Daubeny.
Drawing by William Hart Baxter.

FACING 1840s University plan of the Garden showing a proposed arrangement for glasshouses Daubeny wanted to build, plus the arrangement of beds in the walled garden and between the Cherwell and the East Wall. Drawn by H.T. Underwood and etched by C. Mathews.

and their maintenance could be crippling.[23] In 1733, the Garden responded by commissioning the Oxford-based mason-architect William Townesend (c.1676–1739) to build two, modest, architectural conservatories. The conservatories were evidently well stocked: 'there are about 900 exotics in pots, with large stoves and greenhouses. Among the exotics are Coffee, Tea, Cotton tree, Sugar cane ... Pine apples'.[24] However, growing the exotic came at a price; the conservatories consumed approximately 40 per cent of the Garden's annual recurrent budget between 1735 and 1754.[25]

Architectural conservatories proved more decorative than practical plant accommodation. By the end of the eighteenth century, the eastern conservatory had become the herbarium, library and lecture room.

In 1853, the western conservatory was converted to the herbarium. The eastern and western architectural conservatories are now Grade 1-listed and Grade 2-listed buildings, respectively.[26] At about the same time as the conservatories were built, two large, more practical, wood-and-glass, lean-to-type glasshouses were erected either side of the Danby Gate.

Maintaining a garden, especially a formal garden, is an expensive undertaking; generations of people responsible for the Garden have had to fight hard for funding. When he bequeathed the University the advowson of Kirkdale (Yorkshire), Danvers probably believed its income would be sufficient to support the Garden.[27] Inevitably, this was not the case, so, in the early eighteenth century, William Sherard devised another scheme to fund the Garden. He endowed the Sherardian Chair of Botany on three strict conditions.[28] The German botanist Johann Dillenius (1684–1747)[29] was to be the first Sherardian Professor. Subsequent incumbents were to be elected by the College of Physicians, not the University. The University would give £150 (£17,700 in 2015) per year to the Garden. The University readily agreed to Sherard's conditions, keeping its bargain to the letter. The Sherardian Professor has been the academic most closely associated with the Garden's management ever since. Until the mid-eighteenth century the money given to the Garden under the terms of Sherard's will held its value, but by the 1800s it had lost half its value and by the 1920s was barely worth having. High maintenance costs and no money for additional investment saw the eighteenth-century glasshouses decay. By 1834, the Garden's accommodation for exotic plants was once again dangerous and inadequate, reflecting badly on the University and its Garden. By 1943, the Garden's finances had shrunk to such an extent that the Sherardian Professor even made public appeals for funding.[30]

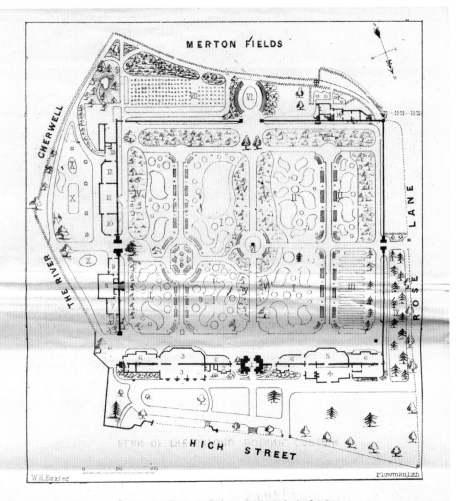

PLAN OF THE OXFORD BOTANIC GARDEN.

EXPLANATION.

BUILDINGS.

1. Entrance Gateway
2. Porters Lodge.
3. Professors House.
4. Chemical Laboratory
5. Room containing the Fielding Herbarium
6 6 6 6, Greenhouses.
7. Orchid House.
8. Victoria Regia House.
9. Fernery.
10. Orangery or Conservatory.
11. Stove House.
12. Seed Room &c.
13. Work Shed &c.
14. Gardener's House.

GROUND.

I. Exotic Herbaceous Plants grouped according to the Natural System.
II. British Herbaceous Plants classed according to the Linnæan System.
III. Exotic Annuals.
IV. British Trees & Shrubs.
V. Exotic Trees & Shrubs.
VI. Centre & Lower Aquariums.
VII. Grass Garden bordered with Medicinal Plants.
VIII. Salicetum.
IX. Pinetum.
X. Spaces for Greenhouse Plants during Summer.

NB. The borders are filled with Miscellaneous Plants, and the Shaded Beds with ornamental plants

Layout of Daubeny's Garden in 1853 following additions of the glasshouses between the East Wall and the Cherwell. Note William Hart Baxter's confusion over east and west.

Revitalization

*the little Regard for Exotick Plants is chiefly owing to the Difficulties
which Gentlemen have met with in preserving them in the Winter*

Bradley (1718) *New improvements of planting and gardening*

WHEN CHARLES DAUBENY (1795–1867)[1] took over as Sherardian Professor in 1834 he had the nucleus of a fighting fund for the Garden's restoration; George Williams (*c.*1762–1834), his predecessor, had bequeathed £500 (£33,900 in 2015) to the Garden. Daubeny soon raised £2,974 8s 10d (£220,000 in 2015) from University sources and private subscribers to fund a new hot house, a porter's lodge and a new professor's house (and lecture room), repairs to the superintendent's house and construction of two concrete garden pools.[2]

Daubeny had the north–south hedges removed, leaving only a pair of Bobart the Elder's original yew trees, and the Garden was planted according to the Linnaean Sexual System to the east and De Candolle's then modern Natural System to the west of the central path.[3] This complex arrangement with its many narrow beds must have been aesthetically displeasing and difficult to maintain. Furthermore, it was retrograde given Linnaeus's system was scientifically redundant. Daubeny soon realized the mistake and had a radical design by the superintendent William Baxter (1787–1871)[4] planted.[5] Baxter's beds were picturesque and curved, making the whole Garden more appealing for a general public. The contents of Daubeny's concrete pools complemented water plants being grown under glass, reflecting historic interests in aquatic plant cultivation.[6] Daubeny also introduced ornaments, for example, the vase that is, today, near the bog garden.[7] However,

FACING Inside Daubeny's Lily House, looking north-west.
Albumen silver print made by Roger Fenton in 1859.

Baxter's picturesque Garden in 1885, looking from the south-east towards the Danby Gate. Woodcut.

FACING Charles Daubeny, fifth Sherardian Professor, who transformed the appearance and fortunes of the Garden in the early nineteenth century. Oil painting.

medicinal plants were consigned to a plot outside the walled garden; perhaps reflecting Daubeny's desire to dispense with old connections.[8]

GLASSHOUSES

Daubeny had a stove house (heated glasshouse) built on the site of the present conservatory in 1835. He was proud of being able to grow a limited selection of 'diminutive' palms, bananas and orchids,[9] but he had greater ambitions.

In 1801 the Bohemian botanist Thaddäus Haenke (1761–1816) discovered the Amazonian water lily, an impressive floating plant with leaves over 2 m across and aromatically scent flowers some 40 cm in diameter. In the 1840s viable seeds were sent back to Britain. Reports of the plant's appearance had been exciting wealthy gardeners for more than a decade; the race was on to be the first to get this plant to flower in Britain.[10] Joseph Paxton (1803–1865), gardener at Chatsworth House, had been experimenting with greenhouse design for decades when, in 1849, he managed to get the giant Amazonian water lily to flower; his horticultural reputation was assured.[11] Daubeny wanted the water lily so in 1851, he rearranged the space outside the East Wall and constructed two ranges of glasshouses either side of the East Gate.

The Lily House tank (8.2 m x 6.4 m x 1.2 m deep), heated by hot-water flowing through iron pipes, was the centrepiece of Daubeny's glasshouse complex; an unpopular one shilling (£4 in 2015) charge for non-University members was made to enter.[12] The Amazonian water lily flowered for the first time in the Garden in 1853; needless to say, it proved a sensation.[13] As the century progressed, the tank brought enormous prestige to the Garden, but the Amazonian water lily was soon discovered to take up a disproportionate amount of space that could be better used for a superb collection of water lilies. However, one unfortunate and unexpected effect of the tank was a localized increase in malaria incidence, which meant that Garden staff had to be dosed with quinine. Today, mosquito larvae are eaten by the tank's fish.[14]

FACING The Amazonian waterlily grown by Joseph Paxton at Chatsworth in 1849. Dried, vertical section of one of the flowers Paxton raised.

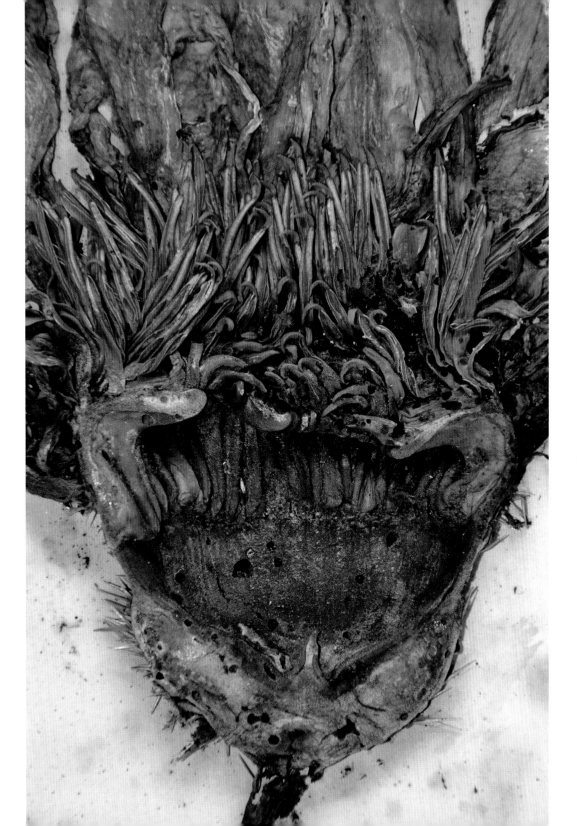

Charles Daubeny's economic waterlily and orchids houses erected in 1851, together with the conservatory built using George William's bequest in 1835. Photograph taken between 1892 and 1894.

Magdalen College and Bridge

Postcard of palm and waterlily houses and conservatory in 1906.
The houses had been rebuilt on the sites of Daubeny's original houses in 1893.

Waterlily house and Daubeny's tank, looking north-west, late 1890s to early c.1905.

BOTANIC GARDENS, ROCKERY, OXFORD. (331)   220368·J.

Rock garden and lower pool in the late 1920s, looking north-west, before the majority
of the Lower Garden was leased from Christ Church College.

Among the aquatic collection was the hybrid known as Daubeny's water lily, which originated in the Garden in about 1851, and is admired for its long-lasting, scented flowers. The American lotus first flowered in the garden in 1852 but, unknown to Daubeny, the first dried specimen of this plant, collected and illustrated by the English collector Mark Catesby, had been in the herbarium since in 1722.[15] Ancient bones, ordure and river silt proved poor foundations for Daubeny's tank, causing it to subside.

The maintenance programme became a burden on the Garden and was eventually funded from Daubeny's own pocket.[16] In the end, however, the subsidence problem was solved as the tank's foundations were improved, the tank remains one of the highlights of a visit to the Garden's glasshouses.

Daubeny's houses had places for ferns, economic plants, insectivorous plants and arid region plants, just as the houses do today. The desert candle in the Arid House was in Daubeny's arid collection, and is one of the Garden's oldest glasshouse plants. A cactus in Daubeny's house, the old man cactus, said to be several hundred years old, died in the early 1880s after the roof of its home was raised to accommodate it: 'his shrivelled skin in the museum is 15 ft. long'.[17] This cactus was not the first, or the last, large, venerable specimen lost or stunted during cycles of glasshouse refurbishment or because of lack of headroom.

AFTER DAUBENY

Charles Daubeny was succeeded by Marmaduke Alexander Lawson (1840–1896) in 1868 but he made no lasting changes to Daubeny's legacy. Lawson was the first Sherardian Professor to resign rather than die in office or retire. Isaac Bayley Balfour (1853–1922),[18] the shortest-serving Sherardian Professor, appointed in 1884, had one of the longest-lasting impacts on the walled garden's appearance. In the 1880s, he swept away the Baxters' curvaceous beds, planting 'order beds' according to George Bentham and Joseph Hooker's arrangement of plant families and genera. At least one person, of course, thought this a 'disaster'.[19] During the twentieth century, academics argued the merits of different classification systems

FACING Portrait of the black pine that dominated the walled garden until it was removed in 2014. Watercolour by botanical artist Rosemary Wise, co-founder of the Oxford University Botanic Garden and Harcourt Arboretum Florilegium Society.

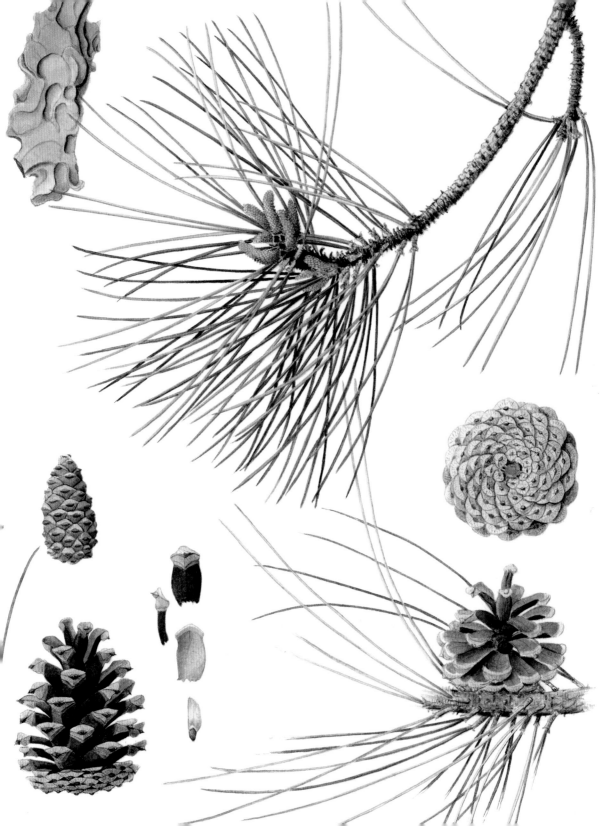

but the order beds remained virtually unchanged. In 1924, Frederick Keeble (1870–1952)[20] made his mark by building a rock garden outside the Walled Garden just beyond the South Gate.[21]

Four significant events marked the Garden during the Second World War. The Garden's longest-serving superintendent, William Baker (1861–1945), was required to retire after 54 years' service. The new Superintendent, George Robinson (1898––1976), laid out the herbaceous border running almost the full length of the South Wall, east of the gate.[22] Three acres (c.1.2 ha) of unprepossessing, flood-prone land was leased from Christ Church, extending the Garden to its present size.[23] Two women were employed as gardeners, although the first woman to have a formal position in the Garden appears to have been the anonymous porteress, guardian of the Library keys in 1835.[24]

Baker's retirement precipitated a shameful episode in the Garden's history. Baker took exception to being asked to retire in 1942 and, in an apparent fit of pique, destroyed many of the Garden's planting records.[25] The Garden's governing body chose to ignore a warning about the risk to the Garden's records in 1918.[26] At best, such indifference speaks of a lack of vision and confidence in the long-term value and scientific role of the Garden. A vast portion of history and scientific data about the Garden was wiped out. Consequently, we have much to rediscover about the Garden and its collections. For example, in 2014, when the Austrian pine, known as 'Tolkien's tree', was felled, an inadequately capped, unknown Victorian well was discovered and the presumed origins of the tree were found to be a myth.[27]

POST-WAR CHANGES

More positively, for more than seventy years, Robinson's herbaceous border has been a source of delight, whilst the extension of the Garden meant new planting ideas could be tried outside the wall garden's formality. By 1947, taking advantage of the Lower Garden's propensity to flood, a 'swamp garden' had been created, whilst a collection of carefully chosen shrubs shielded the Garden from the river.[28]

The Lower Garden has continued to be a site of horticultural innovation, although the bog garden, herbaceous border and rock garden have been constant features since the mid-twentieth century. Today, the innovative and controversial Merton Borders divide opinion, as they do the Lower Garden. The

Borders are innovative because of the planting scheme and their establishment and management methods. They are controversial because of the swathe of 'dead space' they present to visitors during the winter months.

Few people, however, deny the Borders are spectacular complements to Robinson's herbaceous border during the summer months.

Since 1851, glasshouses have been rebuilt approximately every four decades, with generations of staff patching them up between rebuilds. Daubeny's glasshouses, rebuilt in 1894 (cost £2,200; c.£181,000 in 2015), were showing their age by the First World War. Horticultural staff tried to maintain plant collections as the houses deteriorated during the interwar period. By 1949, replacement glasshouses were essential; their total cost was £6,713 (£265,000 in 2015). The glasshouses were replaced once again in 1971.

SIX

Expansion

All Plants which Europe's Fields contain;
For Health, for Pleasure, or for Pain:
Delightful scientifick Shade!
For Knowledge, as for Pleasure made.

Evans (1713) *Vertumnus*

DURING THE NINETEENTH CENTURY, the walled Garden, and even the glasshouses, became too small for the ambitions of its superintendents and professors. For superintendents, location limited the plants they could grow. For the professors, the ways in which plant sciences research and teaching were now done meant different and better facilities were needed.

In 1824, the Austrian botanist Josef August Schultes (1773–1831) was damning: 'the active gardener [William Baxter] ... finding it impossible to make the garden such as he could wish ... cultivates between four and five thousand species of plants in the wretched houses of this garden ... the Oxford Garden is inadequate to the purposes of botanical instruction'.[1]

HERBARIUM AND LIBRARY

The Garden's herbarium and library, which the Bobarts considered essential complements to the living collection, were their personal property. This changed in the 1720s when Bobart the Younger and William Sherard bequeathed their herbaria and libraries to the University. Unusually, personal herbaria had become public property.[2] During the eighteenth century, the Bobart and Sherard herbaria were augmented with the collections of subsequent Sherardian Professors, including

Bookplate designed by Mrs Emery Walker and presented to the Fielding Curator,
George Claridge Druce, by members of the Botanical Exchange Club on 25 June 1925.
The plate depicts the Danby Gate together with elements signifying Druce's interests and
professional and civic life as a botanist, pharmacist and local politician.

Johann Dillenius and John Sibthorp, plus large personal collections, for example, Charles du Bois's (1656–1740) herbarium. By the end of the century, the University possessed a herbarium that was rivalled only by Sir Hans Sloane's (1660–1753) collection which had founded the British Museum.[3]

Space for a herbarium had been created in the eastern conservatory, but this was eventually needed for other things, so the herbarium was evicted. Daubeny chose to have a 'Room for Seeds & Herbarium',[4] which backed onto a garden shed, erected on the banks of the Cherwell (approximately where the Palm House is today). In 1852, he convinced the University to accept the herbarium and library of Henry Fielding (1805–1851).[5] Fielding had spent much of his inherited fortune accumulating one of largest personal herbaria in the Victorian world. Overnight, Fielding's herbarium tripled the size of the Garden's herbarium, thrusting it once again into the top rank of the world's collections. The Fielding Herbarium got a new home in the converted western conservatory.[6] The first Fielding Curator, Maxwell Masters (1833–1907), was appointed in 1853, but resigned after about three years. Subsequent care of the herbarium was sporadic. No Fielding Curator was appointed again until 1886, when Selmar Schönland (1860–1940) arrived, but he remained in post for only three years. The post was vacant until George Claridge Druce (1850–1932) became honorary curator in 1895.[7] Druce worked largely unsupervised and was Curator for the next 37 years; he was probably tolerated because he was well known, wealthy and funded much curatorial work from his own resources. However, little scientific use was made of the herbarium other than emphasizing the prestige of its ancestry. With no one to look after it, the conditions under which specimens were kept had deteriorated; curation was only taken seriously under Druce's stewardship.

Specimens that would not fit into the herbarium were used by Daubeny and William Baxter to create a botanical museum in the room above the Western Conservatory that abutted onto Magdalen College's Chemical Laboratory.[8] The Museum included hundreds of items such as 'an electrotype *Echinocactus*', models of German fungi and 68 types of cinchona bark from across the genus's range.[9] However, the cost of running the museum proved too much, and interest dwindled; the vast majority of the specimens are now lost. Even the Museum's only catalogue was rescued from rubbish discarded by Sydney Vines (1849–1934) when he retired as Sherardian Professor.[10]

W.A. DELAMOTTE DEL.   O. JEWITT Sc.

Charles Daubeny's house on the North Wall of the Garden, completed in 1835. Hand-coloured print based on Orlando Jewitt's wood engraving, published in Daubeny's first guide to the Garden.

EXPERIMENTAL GARDENS

Daubeny and Baxter made a great professor-superintendent partnership. As champions for formal, science-based agricultural education, they were founding supporters of *The Gardeners' Chronicle*.[11] Daubeny, with his chemical background, was interested in experimenting on plants, particularly investigating the effects of fertilizers on growth, and the practical application of plant science.[12] Within months of taking over the Garden in 1834, Daubeny had laid out an Experimental Garden outside the Garden's eastern wall.[13] The unfenced beds were laid out in a manner reminiscent of the Bobarts' Garden, and by 1850, he was conducting experiments on crops such as barley, buckwheat, flax and turnips.[14] Yet space was restricting Daubeny's experiments, plus he had plans to erect new glasshouses. Consequently, in 1852, he bought a piece of land off the Iffley Road as an experimental plot.[15] Daubeny bequeathed the land to the University but his baton in experimental agriculture was never seized, creating 'lost opportunities of half a century'.[16] Without Daubeny's enthusiasm, the Garden's first satellite site failed; the plot was sold for housing in 1901.[17]

Next to Daubeny's original Experimental Garden, William Baxter took the opportunity of the poorly drained soils to grow a 'tolerably good' collection of British willows.[18] With development of the glasshouse complex, willows in the collection died, were replanted in other parts of the Garden or translated to the University Parks. However, labels got mixed up and information lost, rendering the whole collection scientifically useless; another lost opportunity.[19]

In 1964, the Garden experimented with another satellite site; the Genetic Garden on the edge of the University Parks, near the heart of the University's science research and teaching. The Garden was the idea of then Sherardian Professor, Cyril Darlington (1903–1981), and formal beds of interspecific hybrids, variegated plants, domesticated crops and plants with variable chromosome numbers were laid out by the Garden superintendent, Kenneth Burras. The purpose of the Garden was to 'show the [genetic] processes by which evolution is known to be occurring in flowering plants'.[20] However, with Darlington's retirement, lack of interest in the Genetic Garden and its high maintenance costs meant this satellite site was abandoned. It was formally incorporated into the University Parks in 1995.

The Garden and Charles Daubeny's fountain, looking from the centre of the
walled garden towards Magdalen Bridge. Steel engraving by John le Keux,
based on a painting by Frederick Mackenzie, published 1836.

Baxter's Japanese pagoda tree felled in 1973, showing the extension to the height of the
North Wall needed to accommodate the eighteenth-century lean-to glasshouses.
The tree was replanted in 1976 by the University's Chancellor, Harold Macmillan.

PINETUM

In the 1830s, Daubeny probably saw potential financial benefits of focusing on novel economic plants, and started to promote cultivation of cone-bearing trees (gymnosperms) for economic and aesthetic reasons.[21] Yet the Garden did not have the space, the right soil or the finance for such an enterprise. Furthermore, the area within the Garden's walls was too precious to be used for experiments with trees, so in 1843 he rented a narrow strip of land between the Garden's western wall and Rose Lane to start his gymnosperm collection (Pinetum).[22] Here Daubeny planted trees such as monkey puzzle, Nootka cypress and Bhutan pine but he made clear that 'as the plot of ground will not accommodate more than thirty species, it had been the design to select at once the hardiest and the most ornamental'.[23] The Pinetum, which allowed Daubeny and Baxter to undertake experimental arboriculture, was constantly changing.[24] Planting changes were forced by biology, the Garden's landlord, Acts of God (such as when temperatures dropped to -18°C on Christmas Eve 1860) or, after Daubeny died, dwindling enthusiasm.[25] Consequently, few of the gymnosperms in the Pinetum reached maturity; only the Corsican pine and Atlantic cedar remain from the original planting.

Daubeny was not alone in wanting to create a Pinetum. In 1835, at Nuneham Courtnay, about eight kilometres south-east of Oxford, on an island of acidic soil, planting of the Nuneham Park estate pinetum started, and as early as 1838 the Garden was getting plants from the estate.[26] In 1949, the University acquired the estate, and 14 years later University authorities were persuaded to retain part of the pinetum as an arboretum.[27] The Arboretum became the Garden's third experiment with a satellite site, and meant Daubeny's vision might be fulfilled, a diverse collection of gymnosperms grown to maturity.

FACING Portrait of Japanese nutmeg-yew, an East Asian gymnosperm at home in the Arboretum. Watercolour by botanical artist Gaye Willcox Norman, a member of the Oxford University Botanic Garden and Harcourt Arboretum Florilegium Society.

SEVEN

Growing Trees

Every one feels that trees are among the grandest and most ornamental objects of natural scenery: what would landscapes be without them?

Loudon, *Arboretum et Fruticetum Britannicum* (1838b)

TREES ARE THE MOST LONG-LASTING, living features of the ever-changing Garden landscape. Despite the Bobarts training and clipping their trees and shrubs, they grew a diverse array of evergreens, including box, juniper and pyracantha.[1] We know little about tree planting in the eighteenth-century Garden, but by the nineteenth century there were four geographically focused tree collections. Today, the white mulberry, hornbeam and buckthorn (all planted *c.*1800) are the sole survivors of the European and British collections, respectively.[2] In addition to these trees and Bobart's yew, three other trees are more than 150 years old – the magnificent service (planted *c.*1795) and whitty pear (planted *c.*1850) trees in the walled garden, and the precarious-looking black walnut (planted *c.*1860) in the Lower Garden. A notable twentieth-century tree addition to the Garden, the dawn redwood, a Chinese 'fossil' gymnosperm discovered in 1941, was planted in 1949 from one of the original Chinese seed collections; one day it may equal the height of Magdalen College Tower.[3]

FACING The Arboretum in the early 1970s.

OVERLEAF The bluebell wood, an example of the opportunities offered for habitat management by the Arboretum.

PAGES 74–75 The acer glade at the Arboretum.

SPACE FOR TREES

In 1911, the walled garden contained more than 100 tree species of various sizes and ages, which was thought too many.[4] When Druce closed his Report of the belated celebrations of the Garden's Tercentenary, he stated the Garden 'was not a fitting home for an Arboretum'.[5] He suggested various sites for an arboretum within the city centre but ignored the planting of unusual trees in the University Parks that had happened since the mid-1860s.[6]

The Garden got its arboricultural opportunity in 1963 when the University handed over 4.6 acres (c.1.9 ha) of the Nuneham Park estate for the Garden to manage.[7] In collaboration with the Professor of Forestry, the then Sherardian Professor, Cyril Darlington, took on the opportunity, even asking the University for more land. Darlington offered to purchase additional land and lease it back to the University at a preferential rate, but this was turned down. By 1965 negotiations for additional land had reopened and Darlington started to fundraise. With considerable external support an additional 27 acres (c.10.9 ha) was acquired in 1968. Since the early 1970s, the Arboretum has gradually grown in area until, in 2006, 50 acres (c.20.2 ha) of land (Palmer's Leys) was purchased with the help of the Friends of the Botanic Garden and Harcourt Arboretum, bringing the total area of the Arboretum site to approximately 130 acres (52.6 ha).[8]

The Garden and Arboretum sites are very different in their histories and physical characteristics. The Garden evolved on a site where souls were laid to rest;

the Arboretum on a site from where souls were evicted.[9] The city centre Garden grew on a cleared site over generations, whilst the Arboretum was carved out of a collection of mature trees, following decades of neglect.[10]

TREES ON SHOW

The nucleus of the Arboretum is the pinetum started by Edward Venables-Vernon-Harcourt (1757–1847), Archbishop of York, in 1835, according to a layout by the landscape designer William Sawrey Gilpin (c.1761–1843), and continued by his grandson William Edward Harcourt (1908–1979).[11] The Archbishop was working within a landscape managed by his family since the 1710s. In the 1770s, Simon Harcourt (1714–1777), the first Earl Harcourt, decided major alterations were necessary to improve the landscape; one alteration included moving his tenants and their village. The second Earl continued landscaping in the 1780s with the help of Lancelot 'Capability' Brown (1716–1783).

The Arboretum now has a superb collection of mature conifers, especially from North America, within a historic landscape, which can be viewed from the top of Windmill Hill. The trees would be impossible to grow in the confines of central Oxford; particularly magnificent specimens include coastal and giant redwoods and incense cedar, which are amongst the oldest trees in the Arboretum.

The impressive collection of acid-loving azaleas, camellias, rhododendrons and stewartias lining the Serpentine Ride, and other ericaceous trees and shrubs across the Arboretum, would be unattainable on Danvers' site. Rhododendrons were a favourite of Victorian shrubberies. At the Arboretum these vivid, late spring and early summer species and hybrids have been collected together from across the world for more than 150 years. With beauty may come the beast; *Rhododendron ponticum* escaped the confines of shrubberies in the early twentieth century to become a serious weed across Britain.[12] Without constant vigilance, *Rhododendron ponticum* once choked areas of the Arboretum, outcompeting other plants and making parts of the site inaccessible.[13]

The Acer Glade, planting of which started in the late 1960s, has a great range of East Asian and North American maple species. It is maples that produce some of the most spectacular displays of autumn colour seen in North American deciduous forests. Briefly, in the autumn, the Glade becomes a tapestry of reds, yellows, oranges and browns as the maples lose their leaves.

MORE THAN TREES

The space at the Arboretum means more than single specimen trees can be planted. Whole populations of a species or entire habitats can be planted or encouraged, with immense conservation benefits. Furthermore, skills needed to manage wooded habitats, such as coppicing and hedge laying, and which use woodland products, such as charcoal burning and construction, are encouraged in the Arboretum. As the name suggests, the Bluebell Wood is a piece of semi-natural oak woodland, carpeted with bluebells in the spring. Management of the woodland for bluebells also conserves other plants and animals typical of Oxfordshire oak woodland; species and habitat conservation hand-in-hand.

A similar approach operates in the Arboretum meadows. Many meadows disappeared from lowland Britain during the 1970s and 1980s as they were ploughed up to increase agricultural production.[14] As part of the Arboretum, the eponymous Pylon Meadow survived these events. It has been managed without fertilizers or herbicides since the early 1960s, and has a high diversity of meadow plants.[15] As an experiment, when Palmers Leys was purchased the decision was made to restore this arable area to meadow by sowing with grassland species.[16] The meadows are at their best in early summer, replete with ox-eye daisies, vetch, clovers, buttercups

Palmers Ley's Meadow at the Arboretum, June 2014.

and yellow rattle. Grassland has been an essential part of the landscape around the Arboretum since the Harcourt family began building its vision of the natural world. Management of the meadows today contributes to species and habitat conservation, as well as conservation of the historic man-made landscape of the former Nuneham Park estate.

In the Garden's history, the Arboretum is a relative newcomer. Planning and planting an arboretum requires confidence and centuries-long vision. In contrast, planning the walled garden involves vision of decades, whilst under glass this may be reduced to years. The Archbishop's trees have matured in a landscape, and environment, rather different to that which he envisaged. Plants collected together as expressions of power and influence are today part of species conservation programmes that emphasize involvement by everyone. High-technology environmental monitoring reduces the hit-and-miss nature of long-term planting judgements. Today, additions to the Arboretum (and Garden) collections are made after careful consideration of provenance and the likely benefits to overall strategy. The Arboretum is not only beautiful; it has immense strategic value, as Darlington recognized. It is the site upon which the Garden can expand during the twenty-first century to meet ever-changing public, teaching and research needs.

Aloë Africana macu- lata, spinosa minor.

EIGHT

Engaging People

Yet sons of Adams venture not too near,
Nor pluck forbidden fruit, if with intent
To visit Paradise be innocent.

Drope, *Upon the most Hopefull ...* (1664) in Gunther (1912)

THE MODERN GARDEN has three remits: teaching, public engagement and research. The Garden was open to the public from the first; 'serviceable ... to persons of all qualitie serving to help ye diseased and for ye delight & pleasure of those of perfect health ... plants for ye honor of our nation and Universitie & service of ye Com[m]onwealth'...[1] However, in the early eighteenth century, the 'public' was redefined implicitly as the collegiate university;[2] the lack of interest in a wider public was not unusual for the period.

THE RULES

The eighteenth-century garden would have been an imposing sight with its high walls and locked gates. This was not helped by the Garden's seven rules;[3] six restricted visitors, only one placed an obligation on the garden. Visitors were not to 'break through, or leap over the Hedges and Fences', be 'within the *Quarters* or close *Walks* of the Garden' without the professor or gardener, be a woman, have a dog and damage or deface the plants or buildings. The only obligation on

FACING *Aloe maculata* from Johann Dillenius's *Hortus Elthamensis* (1732), drawn, engraved and coloured by the author. The plant was part of James Sherard's collection at Eltham Palace that eventually became part of the Garden's celebrated succulent collection in the late eighteenth century.

the Garden staff was to be available from opening to closing time. These rules were evidently malleable; dogs and women appear in early Garden engravings.[4] Furthermore, the rules did not appear to preclude the aeronaut and chemist James Sadler (1753–1828) from making one of the first English balloon ascents from the Garden on 12 November 1784.[5]

Visitors welcome to the Garden passed between a pair of yew trees, clipped into the forms of armed giants, just inside the Danby Gate.[6] These guardians of the Garden's treasures attracted public attention but were also reminiscent of statutes of Priapus, a minor god of fertility, used to protect Roman gardens.[7] The Garden's academic public, no doubt aware of the allusion, still needed reminding theft was wrong. A printed sheet survives in the archives that states: 'No *Roots*, Plants, Flowers, Fruits, Seeds. Slips, *Cuttings* or *Specimens* of *Plants* are to be given, sold, exchanged or taken away, without special Leave from the PROFESSOR'.[8]

In 1883, one light-fingered Garden guide was fined 10 shillings (c.£98 in 2015) for the 'wilful plucking of flowers'.[9]

In 1835, Daubeny's new rules were at least as restrictive as those they replaced;[10] the Garden was open to 'Members of the University', the entrance was locked and visitors had to 'ring the Bell', conservatories and greenhouses were only unlocked on application and 'General orders have been given to exclude Nursery-maids and Children from the Premises'. Patronizingly, entry would be allowed to those for whom entry 'may seem to be a source of interest or improvement'. However, Daubeny did write the first popular guide to the garden in 1850 and made it his business to involve the garden with city-based horticultural organizations, for example, an annual winter exhibition of chrysanthemum varieties.[11]

In 1887, the Gardens began opening on Sundays, between midday and six o'clock, during the summer, with a member of the local constabulary on duty to discourage misbehaviour.[12] By 1912, the rules had been reduced to three lines, including the delightfully cryptic 'Children are not admitted unless in charge of a responsible adult'.[13] Today, the Garden Rules can be summarized as 'be courteous'; thieves and dogs remain unwelcome.

It was not only visitors who were bound by rigid rules; the Garden's Governing Committee introduced a 'Gardiner's Oath' in 1735:

FACING Entrance into the Garden through the Danby Arch, 1940.

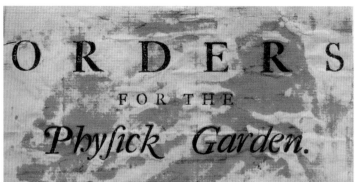

ORDERS

FOR THE

Physick Garden.

I. **THAT** no *Person* presume to break through, or leap over the Hedges and Fences in the *Garden*.

II. That no *Person* appear within the *Quarters*, or close *Walks* of the *Garden*, unless the *Professor* or *Gardiner* attends on such *Person* during his Stay there.

III. That no *Person* brings Dogs into the *Garden*, or do any Damage to the *Green-Houses*, *Stoves*, *Trees* or *Plants*, by Handling, Breaking, or otherways Defacing Them, or by Meddling with any of the *Numbers*.

IV. That no *Person* continue in the *Garden* after the Dusk of the Evening, but depart quietly at the usual Time of Shutting the *Gates*.

V. That no *Person* be admitted in the *Garden* on *Sundays*.

VI. That Attendance be given to such as want to see the *Garden*, *Stoves*, &c. from the Opening of the *Garden Gates* to the Closing of the Same.

VII. No *Roots*, *Plants*, *Flowers*, *Fruits*, *Seeds*, *Slips*, *Cuttings* or *Specimens* of *Plants*, are to be given, sold, exchanged or taken away, without special Leave from the **PROFESSOR.**

The earliest known printed Visitor Rules for entry to the Garden, probably from the early to mid-eighteenth century.

You shall swear that you will truly & faithfully discharge the Office of Gardiner of the Physick Garden in this University so long as you shall therein continue: That you will be obedient to the Professor of Botany and to all such Rules and Order as shall be given You by him (with the Approbation of the Committee: that you will render to him every Week or oftner if required a true and exact Account of all Moneys received by You or any Person under You for shewing the Green-houses, Stoves, or any other Thing belonging to the Garden:) That you will not suffer any Waste or Damage to be made of any Kind whatsoever, nor sell nor permit to be sold any Roots, Plants, Flowers, Fruits, Seeds, or Specimens of Plants, nor give away nor exchange any Thing in the Garden without special Leave from the Professor: & yt you will be diligent in ye Attendance, & in ye Performance of ye dayly Work, & careful in preserving the Plants, Furniture, & Utensils of the Garden, & do every other Thing which is incumbent on a good & skillful Gardiner to do to ye utmost of ye Ability. So help you God.[14]

In 1751, after less than a year at the Garden, Georg Dionysius Ehret (1708–1770) was dismissed for refusing to make his Oath to the Professor, Humphrey Sibthorp.[15] The Oath appears to have been used well into the nineteenth century.

TEACHING

The first formal lecture in the Garden took place on 5 September 1670, when the newly inaugurated Regius Professor, Robert Morison, stood in the centre of the walled garden, behind a table of plants, and talked to his male audience.[16] Morison was an engaging teacher, although his strong Scottish accent marred his eloquence for some ears; 'though a master in speaking and writing the Latin tongue, yet [he] hath no command of the English, as being much spoyled by his Scottish tone'.[17] Once research took over Morison's life, however, his performances became sporadic.

In 1736, the Garden Committee formalized the teaching duties of the Sherardian Professor, who was to 'begin his Lectures about ye middle of March ... once a Week ... till ye End of Aprill ... & twice in ye Week during ye Months May, June, July & August, unless he shall think fit to absent himself on his own or Garden-Affairs ... & then in September to resume his Lecture & read only once a Week till ye Season is entirely over. The Length of ye Lecture to be calculated in Proportion to ye Number of Plants growing in the Garden ... The Days & Hours of demonstrating to be such as the Professor himself shall judge proper'.[18] The Professor was to 'annually open his Lectures in ye Spring with a short Speech in Latin ... close them in ye same Manner in Autumn & also make a Botanick Harangue once every Year in ye Physick School'. Furthermore, fieldwork was to be undertaken 'betwixt ye Middle of April & ye latter End of September make an Herborization once a Fortnight ... in ye Countrys about Oxon, as also twice at least in each summer shall make some further Excursions to collect scarce and rare English Plants for ye Garden'. However, prudently, the University was to be 'at no Expence for or in Relation to any such Herborization'.

Despite these requirements, the nadir of the Garden's teaching (and research) came during Humphrey Sibthorp's 37-year tenure of the Sherardian chair; he gave one unsuccessful lecture and published nothing.[19] Sibthorp flirted with research soon after his appointment but rapidly became the Garden's quiescent centre.[20] Famously, in 1764, the future intellectual architect of the Royal Botanic Garden Kew, Joseph Banks (1743–1820), arrived in Oxford keen to study botany; he looked at what was on offer and sent to Cambridge for a tutor.[21] By 1776, the Professor's lethargy was the subject of University gossip: 'whatever Opinion People may have of the general Establishment of the Physic Garden and Botany Professorship as a Burden on the University ... they cannot now get rid of it'.[22]

Sibthorp's son, John, went to Scotland for his medical training and became fascinated with Linnaeus's new approach to plant classification; evidently his father's traditional approach had failed to inspire.[23] Humphrey eventually resigned as Sherardian Professor in his son's favour; John went off to Europe on a study tour and returned to Oxford in 1787. This tour included Sibthorp's famous exploration of the eastern Mediterranean that eventually led to the publication of the *Flora Graeca* (1806–1840), one of the world's most fabulous plant books.

Despite appearances, John Sibthorp proved to be a dedicated teacher; 'In respect to Myself no less from my Inclination than my duty ... I shall be happy to meet the Wishes & direct the Enquiries of ye. Botanical Student no less in the Time of Vacation than in the Hour of Lecture'.[24] Between c.1788 and 1793 John gave an annual series of 30 lectures in the Garden.[25] His students (presumably all male) were evidently interested in medicine and agriculture, and through Sibthorp's anecdote-laced lectures, we learn much of his adventures in the eastern Mediterranean and his interest in experimental botany.[26]

FACING Robert Morison, the first Professor of Botany in a British University, and the intellectual foundation of the early Garden. Oil painting.

John Sibthorp, third Sherardian Professor and late eighteenth-century
explorer of the eastern Mediterranean. Oil painting.

FACING Olive collected by John Sibthorp in the eastern Mediterranean in the late 1780s.
Watercolour by Ferdinand Bauer, used by Sibthorp as a teaching aid in his undergraduate lectures.

Garden labels from the early eighteenth century to the present day. The earliest labels were numbered lead markers (bottom right); they appear to have been used until the end of the eighteenth century. During the nineteenth and twentieth centuries there were experiments with different types of labels, for example, lead, porcelain and clay, slate, cast iron and write-on metal labels. Today, plastic laminates are used.

During George Williams' tenure as Professor, he advertised lecture courses, but it was the Garden superintendent William Baxter who took eager responsibility for the botanical teaching.[27] Baxter took the same role under Charles Daubeny. Daubeny was a prolific teacher and enthusiastic promoter of science teaching, but apparently 'could not condescend to rudimentary teaching'.[28] During the early twentieth century, teaching became more formalized and the Garden a regular source of material for lectures and practical classes.

SUPPORTING CHANGE

Despite his Rules, Daubeny tried to make the Garden more welcoming to visitors. William Baxter removed the Garden's formality, making it more picturesque and giving it the appearance of a Victorian public park. The eccentric Daubeny introduced monkeys, presumably marmosets or macaques, to the Danby Arch, which sometimes escaped their cages.[29] On Daubeny's death, the monkeys were auctioned, and eventually dissected by the Linacre Professor of Anatomy and Physiology.[30] Despite all of Daubeny's efforts, when geologist John Phillips (1800–1874) wrote Daubeny's obituary in 1868, he thought there was still little to attract Oxford's citizens into the Garden.[31]

Informing visitors about the plants in the Garden has moved a long way from the numbered labels used during the Bobarts' and Dillenius's time,[32] or the scientific names 'printed in legible Characters on labels affixed to the Plants'[33] by John Sibthorp. Daubeny appears to have tried pottery labels with a scientific name, common name and distribution information.[34] Today's plastic plant labels have similar information, but permanent visitor interpretation remains a sensitive issue.

The Garden has benefited from the generosity of supporters and patrons since its inception. Danvers' original gift leased the land and built the fabric. William Sherard dramatically enhanced the quality of glasshouses in the eighteenth century, whilst his bequest forced the University to provide limited financial support to the Garden. James Sherard (1666–1738) and Adrian Haworth's (1768–1833) plant donations created the finest European collections of succulents for more than a century. In 1882 it was transferred to Kew: the Editor of the *Gardeners' Chronicle* stated 'one cannot help regretting the transfer of the unique collections ... the step may have been necessary – of that we cannot judge – but we may nevertheless regret that it was'.[35] Earlier in the nineteenth century, George Williams' bequest, and subscribers to Daubeny's request for funds, effectively created a new Garden.

In 1991 the organization the Friends of the Botanic Garden and Arboretum was formed to support the Garden's activities. The Friends provide important project-based funding and an external view of the Garden; they are 'friendly critics'. In 2006, the only purpose-built staff accommodation in the Garden's history and one of the most significant building projects undertaken in the Garden's modern history, the Charlotte Building, was made possible through generous supporters.[36]

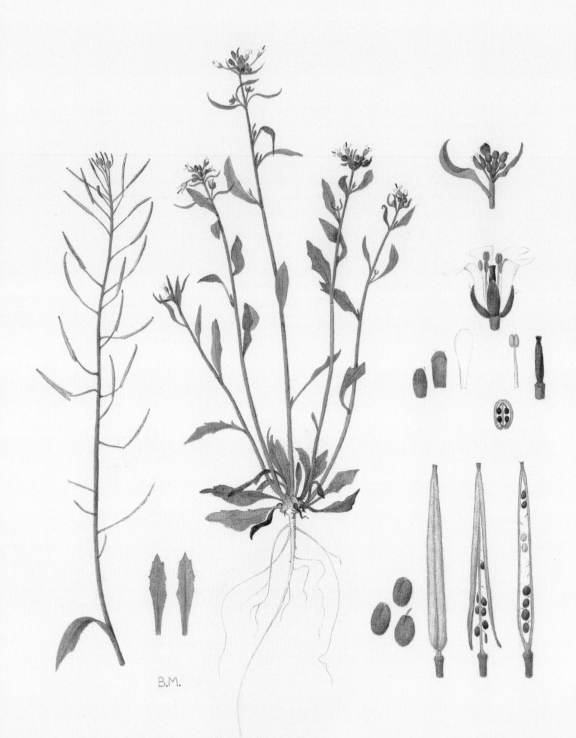

B.M.

NINE

Pursuing Science

the Naturalist ought to feel, that when the name of his plant has been
ascertained, the scientific portion of his task is yet to be begun

Daubeny (1853), *Address to the Members of the University*

V AST AMOUNTS OF MONEY are spent on plant biology research and teaching annually. Why? At its simplest, the answer is because plants are fundamental to our lives; they provide us with food and medicine – even the air we breathe.[1] More than 2,000 years ago, the Greek philosopher Theophrastus justified his botanical interests in similar utilitarian terms.[2] More fundamentally, we are curious about the world around us. Experimental evidence for fundamental aspects of plant biology emerged at various times during the Garden's history: the plant cell in 1665, plant sexual reproduction in 1694, water movement in 1720s, and photosynthesis in 1779.[3] The Garden played no direct part in any of these botanical milestones, but there was no shortage of curiosity.[4]

When the Garden was founded we understood little of how plants work, and had yet to develop a universal vocabulary for communicating about them.[5] Questions about plants need answers from observation, description, experiment and modelling, drawing upon data from scientific collections, fieldwork, laboratory work and cultivation. Unfortunately, different approaches to understanding plant biology have frequently been unproductively pitted against each other.

Charles Daubeny saw the study of plants as a pure and applied discipline in its own right; it was more than a mere handmaid to medicine.

FACING Portrait of thale cress, a weedy species that has become a model plant since the 1980s. Watercolour by botanical artist Barbara McLean, co-founder of the Oxford University Botanic Garden and Harcourt Arboretum Florilegium Society.

In 1834, just over a month after his appointment to the Sherardian Chair, Daubeny subtly signalled the Garden was changing. When he addressed the Royal College of Physicians he began using 'Physic Garden' but within a few paragraphs was referring to the 'Botanic Garden'; the name stuck.[6] 'Botanic Garden' summarized his philosophical and practical view of university science and education.[7]

In his 1953 Inaugural Lecture, the newly appointed Sherardian Professor of Botany, Cyril Darlington, a gifted, pioneering plant geneticist, was adamant the Garden's focus on taxonomic research was to the detriment of plant sciences.[8] Darlington blamed William Sherard for bequeathing the University 'the finest herbarium in Europe' and the University for accepting the terms of Sherard's will and selling Daubeny's fledgling experimental station.

CATALOGUING DIVERSITY

The 1648 and 1658 Catalogues were the Garden's first scientific publications. Robert Morison's book on the carrot family, *Plantarum umbelliferarum distributio nova* (1672) heralded much greater scientific ambitions; *Plantarum historiae universalis Oxoniensis* (1680, 1699), a new classification of the world's plants to be published in three volumes. Morison's *Plantarum umbelliferarum*, the first illustrated botanical monograph, focused on a plant group rather than plants from a geographic region. Furthermore, it included a method that is now the universal approach to formal plant identification; the botanical key. The *Plantarum historiae* proved to be an extremely expensive, poorly conceived and managed publication, and was never completed.[9] Morison got sponsorship for some of the elaborate copper engravings but with a meagre annual professorial salary, augmented by a royal salary that was frequently in arrears, the project brought him to the brink of penury.[10] Scientifically, Morison's work was eclipsed by that of his Essex-based academic rival John Ray (1627–1705).[11]

The work of Johann Dillenius, whom William Sherard insisted be the first Sherardian Professor, was also plagued by the expense of illustrations; Dillenius's solution was to learn to engrave. He is best known for *Hortus Elthamensis* (1732),

FACING Mandrake watercolour painted by Ferdinand Bauer in Oxford from sketches made during John Sibthorp's exploration of the eastern Mediterranean in the late 1780s.

Atropa Mandragora

Copper plate of cereals, etched by Michael Burghers, used to print illustrations
in Robert Morison's *Plantarum historiae universalis Oxoniensis* (1699).

FACING Lichen specimens used by Johann Dillenius for illustrating his *Historia Muscorum* (1741).
The sheet border is eighteenth-century wallpaper. Note the twentieth-century labels, illustrating
the continued scientific importance of specimens collected hundreds of years ago.

Parmelia exasperata (Ach.) deNot.

P.w James   VIJ 1958.

C. E Be-
tulis, Charl
ton wood.

E Luercubus juncoribus
prope Heddington.

Cum glomerulis granu-
lolis, similibus figuræ Mich T. 51. Ord. XIX.

XXIV. 77. Lichenoides olivaceum, fcutellis lævibus. *The*
A. B. f.   *Olive colour'd Lichenoides, with fmooth Plates.*

melia *syntype of P. olivacea*
is Ctred   **B. C —**

det. Mason E. Hale, Jr., U. S. National Museum   1961

B.   *Parmelia exasperata. (Ach.) de*N.

Det. P.w James.   XI 1967

Parmelia fuliginosa
var betervirens

P.w James   VII 1961

olivaceum, fcutellis amplioribus
Olive colour'd Lichenoides, with

warty Difhes.

79.

79. Lichenoides acetabulis
cutaneis & rugofis. *The Olive*
colour'd Lichenoides, with
wrinkl'd Bowles.

melia — *lectotype of*
P. omphalodes (L.) Ach.

det. Mason E. Hale, Jr., U. S. National Museum

80 C
Typotype
3. on f 1993
PwJ
1961

80. Lichenoides faxatile tinctorium, foliis pilofis XXIV
purpureis *Syn. St. Brit. III. p.*74. *n.*70.   Cork or   **A. B. C.**

an illustrated folio of the plants growing in James Sherard's garden, including the succulents that made the Garden's eighteenth-century horticultural reputation. Dillenius's most scientifically enduring and original work was the *Historia Muscorum* (1741), a description of algae, mosses, liverworts and lichens.[12] In 1736, Linnaeus visited Oxford specifically to meet Dillenius. Within Linnaeus's hearing, Dillenius is reported to have described him as 'the man who has thrown all botany into confusion'.[13] However, what started as a frosty relationship developed during the week-long visit into a strong, mutual friendship.

Two great botanical artists were fleetingly associated with the eighteenth-century Garden, Georg Dionysius Ehret and Ferdinand Bauer (1760–1826). Ehret had a tense working relationship with Humphrey Sibthorp when he was employed as superintendent in 1751.[14] More famously, but equally tense, Humphrey's son, John, employed Bauer as an artist during his exploration of the eastern Mediterranean.[15] Bauer's watercolours are some the world's finest botanical illustrations and, following John's death, were eventually published as the *Flora Graeca* (1806–1840), one of the rarest and most expensive botanical books ever written.[16] As a consequence of his poor working habits, Sibthorp's contribution to the *Flora* is eclipsed by that of Bauer. Importantly, Sibthorp was fascinated by what experimentation revealed about the life of plants and made a bequest establishing the Sibthorpian Chair of Rural Economy.[17] Botanical illustration has remained important for plant sciences in Oxford, and for over fifty years has drawn on the peerless talents of Rosemary Wise, and more recently the Oxford University Botanic Garden and Harcourt Arboretum Florilegium Society.[18]

FACING Portrait of *Nymphaea* x *daubenyana*, a long-flowering, scented waterlily that arose in the Garden, probably as a cross between the West African N. *micrantha* and the South-East Asian N. *nouchali*. Watercolour by botanical artist Margaret Fitzpatrick, a member of the Oxford University Botanic Garden and Harcourt Arboretum Florilegium Society.

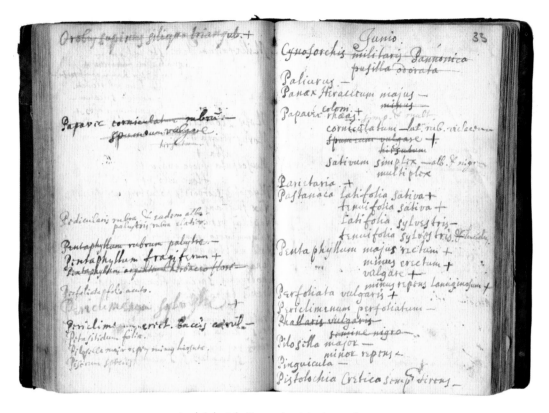

Jacob Bobart the Younger's notebook recording
flowering months of plants growing in the Garden.

HORTICULTURAL RESEARCH

Dried plants are a tantalizing catalogue of life but will not satisfy anyone interested in living plants; for that skilled gardeners are needed. Gardeners, like physicians, developed their skills over thousands of years of trial and error. Yet horticultural knowledge could be looked upon with distain by academics.[19]

The Bobarts were highly skilled, experimental gardeners; they had to be to grow the new plants arriving from North America and propagate them for their illustrious clients. In March 1694, following a visit the younger Bobart made to

98

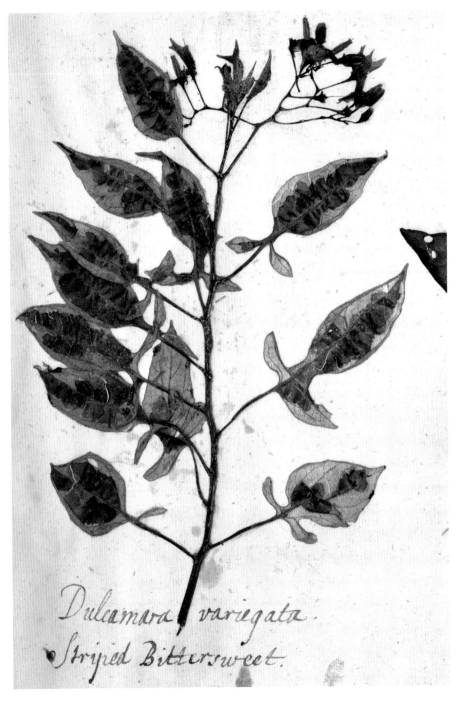

Dulcamara variegata.
Striped Bittersweet.

Striped bittersweet, labelled by Jacob Bobart the Younger and probably collected from the Garden in the 1680s. This plant was introduced to the Garden when Robert Morison arrived in Oxford in 1669.

Mary Somerset (*c*.1630–1715), Duchess of Badminton's celebrated gardens, he tried to sell her some plants: 'I send now a packet of such seeds as to me seem hopefull ... I send allsoe Madam a note of such good plants as I do not remember to have seen in yr Graces plantations.'[20] Jacob Bobart the Younger's catalogues are credited with founding seed exchange schemes, although exchange was established practice among seventeenth-century botanists and gardeners.[21]

The Bobarts were interested in experimenting with anything that might increase income, for example, grafting techniques, nutrient regimes and novel plant selection. Ventures into more philosophical aspects of experimentation proved less successful. For example, in an age of widespread alchemical beliefs, they asserted, with authority given their horticultural reputations, that, if left in the soil, 'Crocus' changed into 'Gladiolus'.[22]

Bobart the Younger's horticultural observations led him to suggest single-flowered and double-flowered carnations could be differentiated before they flowered. If true, 'beautiful and profitable' double forms could be cheaply screened from commonplace single forms.[23] His father, a skilled grafter of trees and vines, is credited with developing a grafting method. He also managed to make the popular 'White Frontiniac' vine fruit early by grafting it onto the 'Parsly' vine;[24] the well-rotted contents of New College's 'house of office' his preferred vine manure.[25] Daubeny revived experimental interest in soil nutrients in the mid-nineteenth century, in combination with a chemical laboratory built by Magdalen College on the Garden's North Wall in 1848.[26]

Botanical novelties increased the Garden's scientific and commercial opportunities. The Garden was well-stocked with favourite ornamentals but the Bobarts were always looking for new plants.[27] Naturally occurring mutations of familiar plants were one source, after all this was the basis of the auriculas they bred with such success. Bobart the Younger grew a white-fruited bramble he had spotted near Oxford.[28] Morison arrived in the Garden with a white-variegated woody nightshade he had discovered at Blois.[29] Gradually, the Garden's collection of variegated plants increased; the Bobarts' additions included a striped sycamore from Magdalen College and variegated privet.[30] Although there were discussions of the bases of variegation, it was not until the 1960s, when the collection comprised several hundred variegated plants, that Darlington and Burras were confident enough to propose a variegation classification system.[31]

Oxford ragwort growing on the churchyard walls of
St Peters-in-the-East, where the Bobarts and Dillenius are buried.

PLANT COLLECTION

Plant collection expeditions are important sources of new plants. Seeds or spores are the easiest means to transport living plants. However, if the Garden was to benefit from new plants, gardeners had to discover how to germinate the seeds, the right conditions to maintain the plants, and eventually how to make them flower and fruit. Furthermore, if plants were to be distributed, the best ways to propagate them had to be discovered. Notes collectors made in the field could help gardeners. In the late 1780s, John Sibthorp returned to Oxford from his eastern Mediterranean explorations with seeds, bulbs and corms for the Garden. Frustratingly, few details of these collections have survived, the plants and any knowledge about their propagation lost through neglect.[32] In 1889, with Sydney Vines' encouragement, William Baker distributed a seed list, beginning an enormous exchange of plants. By 1910, the Garden had distributed nearly 85,000 plants, bulbs and packets of seed by post, and in turn received more than 51,000 plants, bulbs and packets of seed.[33] The mutual information exchange accompanying this flow of diversity was essential for spreading horticultural research, but this was all lost in Oxford when Baker burnt the Garden's archive.

In 1823, Nathaniel Bagshaw Ward (1791–1868), a London physician, solved the challenge of long-distance transportation of living plants by inventing the Wardian Case, a closed, partially glazed box rather like a mobile greenhouse.[34] Wardian Cases were essential before air travel; although by the early twentieth century the Garden's cases were more useful for raising temperamental filmy ferns.[35]

EXPERIMENTING

The sex lives of plants have been a subject of speculation for centuries.[36] The Bobarts made observations relevant to plant sex but never formalized their conclusions. For example, Bobart the Younger found a white campion with flowers that lacked male parts, and he was aware plants such as cannabis had individuals that did and did not produce seed.[37] He is also credited with the recognition of the London plane, which he described as intermediate between the occidental and oriental planes.[38] During the late nineteenth century, horticulturalists at the Garden became experts at water lily cultivation, whilst Oxford's best-known addition to the British flora, the hybrid Oxford Ragwort, has been studied by Oxford-based plant scientists for over 200 years.

In the early 1700s, this unknown Sicilian plant arrived in Oxford,[39] and until the early 1800s, was a novelty confined to the city's walls. The light, parachute-like ragwort fruits are effective dispersal units. Yet to be spread in its new home, Oxford ragwort needed time to adapt, suitable habitats to grow in and a means to escape to Oxford.[40] The 1840s brought the railway. Ragwort took advantage of the industrial disturbance and spread through western Britain. The Second World War created new habitats and eastern Britain was colonized. The species was first described by Carolus Linnaeus based on samples, collected from the walls of either the city or the Garden, sent to him by Dillenius. In the first complete account of Oxford's plants, John Sibthorp failed to recognize the famous ragwort on the city's walls.[41] However, Oxford ragwort is more than merely a weed that happened to leap a garden wall. As we have learnt more and more about its biology, Oxford ragwort has started to be used by researchers interested in manipulating evolutionary processes; it has graduated to becoming one of a handful of model plants.

Experimental horticulture was practised for centuries in the Garden. The Bobarts and Dillenius, enthusiastic sharers of botanical knowledge, contributed to wide scientific networks. To maintain his relationship with James Petiver (c.1665–1718) at the Chelsea Physic Garden, Bobart the Younger was even prepared to sacrifice part of his own herbarium.[42]

Plants from the Garden were used in 1859 as models for the pillar capital carvings in the University Museum of Natural History.[43]

Despite Daubeny's advocacy of evolutionary ideas and experimental biology, formal experimental approaches to plant biology never took off at the Garden; even Darlington had to retreat to the University Parks.

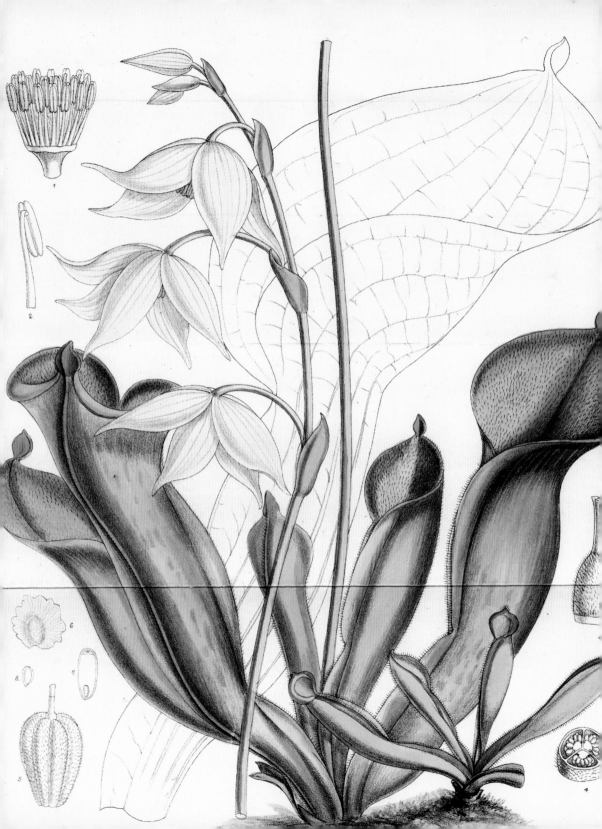

TEN

Splitting Apart

we may expect that the practical wisdom of the garden
and of gardeners will continue to hold together the branching
strands not of one but of several sciences

Darlington (1971), *The Oxford Botanic Gardens: 1621 to 1971*

WHEN DAUBENY formally accepted Fielding's herbarium in 1853 he highlighted its scientific importance and the prestige it brought to the University. Acknowledging the Garden's poor past academic performance, he tried to convince a sceptical audience of the importance of natural science in a University traditionally dominated by the arts and humanities.[1] If academic arguments could not persuade, Daubeny appealed to his audience's self-interest: 'Botany may henceforth be studied in this place without requiring any further augmentation to our existing means of instruction.'

DIVISION

Fewer than twenty years later, the University was faced with a choice. All natural science disciplines, except botany, were clustering around the University Parks, creating a Science Area, and despite Daubeny's optimistic assurance, facilities at the Garden remained inadequate and budgets constantly strained. Consequently, a proposal was made that botany should join her intellectual allies, five acres

FACING Lithograph of *Heliamphora nutans*, originally collected by Robert Schomburgk in 1839 from an Expedition to Mount Roraima, Guyana.

(*c*.2 ha) of the Parks would form a new botanic garden, and the historic site be returned to Magdalen.[2] Joseph Hooker (1817–1911), Director of Kew, was consulted but thought the Garden would cost more to move than to improve. The Sherardian Professor, Marmaduke Lawson, eventually concurred and the University agreed to fund changes to the Garden site; a new Class Room and Laboratory were built and the herbarium modified to a lecture room[3] producing a Department of Botany. The architect of natural science unification, Henry Acland (1815–1900), responded tartly that botany was 'on a leasehold, apart for the rest of the Scientific apparatus of the University'.[4]

By the end of the century the number of students interested in plants had mushroomed, and teaching facilities were once more insufficient.[5] Furthermore, a messy financial arrangement had evolved between the Garden and the fledgling Department of Botany. Micawberesque since the 1640s, by the early twentieth century, finances were based on the uncertainty of hope; professors repeatedly loaning or donating funds to the Garden to keep it afloat.[6]

Continual modification of the existing site was not only inadequate; the landlord was becoming irritated.[7] A solution had to be found. The mood of the University and of the incumbent Sherardian Professor (Theodore Osborn, 1887–1973) had changed[8] – the only practical option for the development of botany in Oxford was to vacate the cramped site. Therefore, if the Garden would not go to the Parks, the Botany Department would go to the new Science Area alone. Plans were laid, a building designed in 1939 and constructed after the Second World War on South Parks Road. On 8 October 1951, the Botany Department officially moved into its new home, which one group of modernist critics called 'excessively formal, unnecessarily symmetrical, stiff and drear'.[9] Vacant buildings at the Garden were returned to Magdalen College and the Garden once again focused on growing plants for teaching and research, and creating a pleasant recreational space.

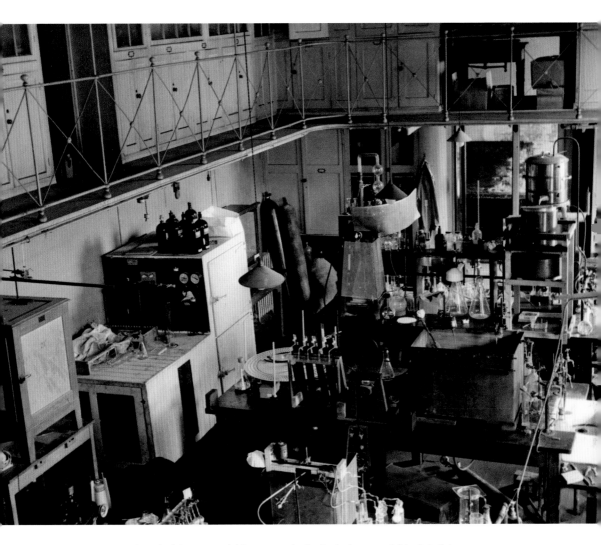

Plant physiology research laboratory at the Garden in the 1940s. Originally built by
Charles Daubeny in 1848 as a lecture room, it was converted to a laboratory in the 1930s.
Today, the room is the Daubeny Lecture Theatre.

Department of Botany (today, Plant Sciences) on South Parks Road, in 1951, from the
south-east; the Herbaria occupies the two floors to the north of the door.

OLD PRINCIPLES IN NEW SKINS

Since the separation of the Garden and the Department of Botany (later the Department of Plant Sciences), the ways plants are studied have changed dramatically. However, the core principles that drove the Bobarts in their development of the Garden remain: grow interesting plants; answer interesting questions about how plants live; and proclaim the importance of plants in our lives.

The latter part of the twentieth century was not just a time for change in the Oxford Garden; botanic gardens worldwide were starting to examine their roles. Until the 1970s, plant conservation merited virtually no consideration at the Garden. Views started to change in the 1980s, and by the 1990s conservation had become a major public and scientific goal of botanic gardens worldwide.[10] Oxford could make major contributions to plant conservation; plant-based education for all age groups was obviously one. Since the 1990s the Garden has been used extensively for enthusing children and adults, outside of the University, about plants and environmental issues. Today, the Garden is regularly used for undergraduate and postgraduate teaching.

The Garden already had a reputation for the conservation of wild plants in cultivation. In 1978, the Garden's superintendent Kenneth Burras collected the unusual insectivorous plant *Heliamphora nutans* on Mount Roraima, Guyana. Garden staff soon became experts at growing these highly collectable plants but found it difficult to stop visitors stealing them. In 1987, collaborating with the University's Forestry Department, an efficient propagation method was discovered. *Heliamphora* could be conserved in the wild, material made available for the horticultural trade and research, and the Garden's displays protected.[11] Collaborations with the Ashmolean Natural History Society's Rare Plants Group have seen the Garden addressing species-based, conservation of Oxfordshire plants.[12] Globally, the Garden and Arboretum are actively involved with North American conifer conservation and science-led conservation of Japanese plants. Collection priorities are also science-led. Plants from known wild sources, with detailed supporting data, are preferred; quality trumps quantity in a small botanic garden.

By the early twenty-first century, broad scientific consensus was reached among botanical researchers on a DNA-based classification of flowering plants. The Garden's horticulturalists were keen to modernize the planting of the Walled Garden from Balfour's late nineteenth-century arrangement. Timothy Walker, the

Garden's Director, supported this view, and took the bold decision to reorganize the Walled Garden; by 2005 the task was complete.[13] Planting of the modern Garden also has two gentle nods to its roots. This includes a collection of plants mentioned in the Garden's first printed catalogue, and a collection of medicinal plants whose inclusion is based on scientific rather than anecdotal evidence.[14]

An unfortunate consequence of Botany Department's move was the separation of the living from the dead; ties among the University's botanical collections started to unravel. However, the herbarium and botanical library got purpose-built homes in the new Department, having been moved from pillar to post for over a century. Furthermore, the Garden's herbaria were joined by the vast personal herbarium of George Druce and the burgeoning herbarium of the Forestry Department, creating one of the largest university herbaria in Europe. The herbarium was finally to be used as Daubeny intended; Druce even made a bequest that funded the staffing of it.

There are few better ways to enthuse people about plants than to immerse them in beautiful, botanically diverse environments such as the Garden and Arboretum. Innovative horticulture and arboriculture can be combined with excellent plant education and research without compromising the Garden and Arboretum's unique recreational qualities.

Few of the world's botanic gardens have a finer setting than that of the Garden in Oxford. The challenge for the Garden's stewards today is to meet the expectations of every user of the Garden and Arboretum within a finite budget.

FACING Portrait of *Euphorbia pasteurii*, named after an Oxford biology undergraduate in 2003. This hybrid, between the critically endangered *E. stygiana* and *E. mellifera*, arose in the Garden and is widely grown in UK gardens. Watercolour by botanical artist Penny Gould, a member of the Oxford University Botanic Garden and Harcourt Arboretum Florilegium Society.

OVERLEAF The Merton Borders in August.

Plant Names

Almond	*Prunus dulcis* (Rosaceae).
Amazonian water lily	*Victoria regia* (Nymphaeaceae).
American agave	*Agave americana* (Asparagaceae).
American lotus	*Nelumbo lutea* (Nelumboaceae).
Anemone	*Anemone* species (Ranunculaceae).
Apple	*Malus pumila* (Rosaceae).
Apricot	*Prunus armeniaca* (Rosaceae).
Asphodeline	*Asphodeline lutea* (Xanthorrhoeaceae).
Atlantic cedar	*Cedrus atlantica* (Pinaceae).
Auricula	*Primula auricula* (Primulaceae).
Austrian pine	*Pinus nigra* subspecies *nigra* (Pinaceae).
Azalea	*Rhododendron* species (Ericaceae).
Barley	*Hordeum vulgare* (Poaceae).
Belladonna	*Atropa belladonna* (Solanaceae).
Bhutan pine	*Pinus wallichiana* (Pinaceae).
Bittersweet	*Solanum dulcamara* (Solanaceae).
Black plum	*Prunus* subgenus *Prunus* (Rosaceae).
Black walnut	*Juglans nigra* (Juglandaceae).
Bluebell	*Hyacinthoides non-scripta* (Asparagaceae).
Box	*Buxus sempervirens* (Buxaceae).
Bramble	*Rubus fruticosus* (Rosaceae).
Buckthorn	*Rhamnus carthaticus* (Rhamnaceae).
Buckwheat	*Fagopyrum esculentum* (Polygonaceae).
Buttercup	*Ranunculus* species (Ranunculaceae).
Camellia	*Camellia* species (Theaceae).
Cannabis	*Cannabis sativa* (Cannabaceae).
Carnation	*Dianthus* species (Caryophyllaceae).
Cherry	*Prunus* subgenus *Cerasus* (Rosaceae).
Chinese magnolia	*Magnolia sieboldii* subspecies *sinensis* (Magnoliaceae).
Christmas cactus	*Schlumbergera* × *buckleyi* (Cactaceae).
Cinchona	*Cinchona* species (Rubiaceae).
Clover	*Trifolium* species (Fabaceae).
Coastal redwood	*Sequoia sempervirens* (Cupressaceae).
Cocoa	*Theobroma cacoa* (Malvaceae).
Coffee	*Coffea* spp. (Rubiaceae).
Corsican pine	*Pinus nigra* subspecies *laricio* (Pinaceae).
Cotton	*Gossypium* species (Malvaceae).
Daubeny's water lily	*Nymphaea* x *daubenyana* (Nymphaeaceae).
Dawn redwood	*Metasequoia glyptostroboides* (Cupressaceae).
Desert candle	*Euphorbia abyssinica* (Euphorbiaceae).
English oak	*Qoercus robur* (Fagaceae).
Fig	*Ficus carica* (Moraceae).
Filmy ferns	Hymenophyllaceae.
Flax	*Linum usitatissimum* (Linaceae).
Giant redwood	*Sequoiadendron giganteum* (Cupressaceae).
Giant reed	*Arundo donax* (Poaceae).
Grass of Parnassus	*Parnassia palustris* (Celastraceae).
Hollyhock	*Alcea rosea* (Malvaceae).

Hornbeam	*Carpinus betulus* (Betulaceae).
Humble plant	*Mimosa pudica* (Fabaceae).
Incense cedar	*Calocedrus decurrens* (Cupressaceae).
Ivy	*Hedera helix* (Araliaceae).
Japanese nutmeg-yew	*Torreya nucifera* (Taxaceae).
Japanese pagoda tree	*Styphnolobium japonicum* (Fabaceae).
Juniper	*Juniperus* species (Cupressaceae).
Lacebark tree	*Lagetta lagetto* (Thymelaeaceae).
Leyland cypress	*Cupressus × leylandii* (Cupressaceae).
London plane	*Platanus x hispanica* (Platanaceae).
Mandrake	*Mandragora officinarum* (Solanaceae).
Maples	*Acer* species (Sapindaceae).
Medlar	*Mespilus germanica* (Rosaceae).
Monkey puzzle	*Araucaria araucana* (Araucariaceae).
Nootka cypress	*Cupressus nootkatensis* (Cupressaceae).
Occidental plane	*Platanus orientalis* (Platanaceae).
Old man cactus	(Cactaceae).
Olive	*Olea europaea* (Oleaceae).
Oriental hyacinth	*Hyacinthus orientalis* (Asparagaceae).
Oriental plane	*Platanus occidentalis* (Platanaceae).
Ox-eye daisy	*Leucanthemum vulgare* (Asteraceae)
Oxford ragwort	*Senecio squalidus* (Asteraceae).
Peach	*Prunus persica* (Rosaceae).
Pear	*Pyrus* species (Rosaceae).
Pineapple	*Ananas comosus* (Bromeliaceae).
Pomegranate	*Punica granatum* (Lythraceae).
Privet	*Ligustrum vulgare* (Oleaceae).
Pyracantha	*Pyracantha* species (Rosaceae).
Quince	*Cydonia oblonga* (Rosaceae).
Rhododendron	*Rhododendron* species (Ericaceae).
Rice	*Oryza sativa* (Poaceae).
Rosemary	*Rosmarinus officinalis* (Lamiaceae).
Sensitive plant	*Mimosa* species (Fabaceae).
Service tree	*Sorbus domestica* (Rosaceae).
Stewartia	*Stewartia* species (Theaceae).
Sugarcane	*Saccharum officinarum* (Poaceae).
Sunflower	*Helianthus annuus* (Asteraceae).
Sycamore	*Acer pseudoplatanus* (Sapindaceae).
Tea	*Camellia sinensis* (Theaceae).
Thale cress	*Arabidopsis thaliana* (Brassicaceae).
Tobacco	*Nicotiana tabacum* (Solanaceae).
Turnip	*Brassica rapa* (Brassicaceae).
Vetch	*Vicia* species (Fabaceae).
Wallflower	*Erysimum cheiri* (Brassicaceae).
Weeping willow	*Salix babylonica* (Salicaceae).
White campion	*Silene latifolia* (Caryophyllaceae).
White mulberry	*Morus alba* (Moraceae).
White plum	*Prunus* subgenus *Prunus* (Rosaceae).
Whitty pear	*Sorbus domestica* (Rosaceae).
Willows	*Salix* species (Salicaceae).
Woody nightshade	*Solanum dulcamara* (Solanaceae).
Yellow rattle	*Rhinanthus minor* (Orobanchaceae)
Yew	*Taxus baccata* (Taxaceae).

Senior Positions in Garden, Plant Sciences and Herbaria

Identity, dates and position held (with dates) for the three principal posts associated with the University's botanical collections.
For positions associated directly with the living collections, impact on the current appearance of the Garden and Arboretum is given.

BOTANIC GARDEN AND ARBORETUM	PROFESSOR	HERBARIUM CURATOR*
Jacob Bobart the Elder (c.1599–1680) Horti Praefectus (1642–1679) Modification: Bobart's yew Died in office	Robert Morison (1620–1683) Danby Professor & Regius Professor (1669–1683) Died in office	
Jacob Bobart the Younger (1641–1719) Horti Praefectus (1679–1719) Died in office [Tilleman Bobart (1662–1724) was Acting Praefectus Horti for a short period in 1717]		
	Edwin Sandys Professor (1720–1724) Retired	
	Gilbert Trowe (d.1734) Professor (1724–1734) Modification: Eastern and western conservatories Died in office	
James Smith Gardener (1738–1749) Unknown	Johann Jacob Dillenius (1684–1747) 1st Sherardian Professor (1734–1747) Died in office	
Georg Dionysius Ehret (1708–1770) Gardener (1750–1751) Dismissed	Humphrey Sibthorp (c.1713–1797) 2nd Sherardian Professor (1747–1784) Retired	
William Stockford Gardener (1752–1753) Dismissed		
Thomas Potts Gardener (1753–1755) Unknown		
John Foreman Gardner (1756–c.1790) Unknown	John Sibthorp (1758–1796) 3rd Sherardian Professor (1784–1795) Regius Professor (1793–1796) Modification: Buckthorn, hornbeam and white	
James Benwell (c.1735–1819) Position unclear although employed in Garden for more than 40 years Retired	mulberry in walled garden Died in office	
	George Williams (c.1762–1834) 4th Sherardian & Regius Professor (1796–1834) Modification: Conservatory site Died in office	
William Baxter (1787–1871) Superintendent (1813–1851) Modification: Appearance of the glasshouses Retired		

BOTANIC GARDEN AND ARBORETUM	PROFESSOR	HERBARIUM CURATOR*
William Baxter (contd)	Charles Giles Bridle Daubeny (1795–1867) 5th Sherardian Professor (1834–1867) 1st Sibthorpian Professor (1840–1867)	
William Hart Baxter (c.1816–1890) Superintendent (1851–1887) Retired	Modification: Glasshouses, especially water lily tank Died in office	Maxwell Tylden Masters (1833–1907) Fielding Curator (c.1853–c.1856) Resigned
	Marmaduke Alexander Lawson (1840–1896) 6th Sherardian Professor (1868–1882) 2nd Sibthorpian Professor (1868–1882) Resigned	
	Isaac Bayley Balfour (1853–1922) 7th Sherardian Professor (1884–1888) Modification: Family bed concept Resigned	Selmar Schönland (1860–1940) Fielding Curator (1886–1889) Resigned
William George Baker (1861–1945) Superintendent (1888–1942) Retired	Sydney Howard Vines (1849–1934) 8th Sherardian Professor (1888–1919) Modification: Buildings at west end of North Wall Retired	George Claridge Druce (1850–1932) Honorary Fielding Curator (1895–1932) Died in office
	Frederick William Keeble (1870–1952) 9th Sherardian Professor (1920–1927) Modification: Rockery Retired	
	Arthur George Tansley (1871–1955) 10th Sherardian Professor (1927–1937) Retired	
	Theodore George Bentley Osborn (1887–1973) 11th Sherardian Professor (1937–1953) Modification: Transfer of Plant Sciences to University Science Area Retired	Nicholas Vladimir Polunin (1909–1997) Acting Fielding Curator (1939) Fielding Curator (1940–1947) Resigned
		John Frederick Gustav Chapple (1911–1990) Druce Curator (1940–1947) Resigned
		Edmund André Charles Louis Eloi Schelpe (1924–1985) Fielding Curator (January–May 1952) Resigned
		Miss S.M. Littleboy Acting Fielding Curator (1953–1956) Unknown
George William Robinson (1898–1976) Superintendent (1942–1963) Modification: Herbaceous border Retired	Cyril Dean Darlington (1903–1981) 12th Sherardian Professor (1953–1971) Modification: Arboretum, Genetic Garden in University Parks, establishment of Plant Sciences Department Retired	Edmund Frederic Warburg (1908–1966) Druce Curator (1948–1956) Druce & Fielding Curator (1957–1966) Died in office
Kenneth Burras Superintendent (1963–1988) Modification: Variegated and carnivorous plant collections Retired		Adrian John Richards Druce Curator (1968–1970) Resigned

BOTANIC GARDEN AND ARBORETUM	PROFESSOR	HERBARIUM CURATOR*
Kenneth Burras (contd)	Robert Whatley 13th Sherardian Professor (1971–1991) Retired	Adrian John Richards (contd)
Timothy Walker Horti Praefectus (1988–2001) Director (2002–2013) Modification: Charlotte Building, APG arrangement of walled garden	Hugh Dickinson 14th Sherardian Professor (1991–2009) Retired	Frank White (1927–1994) Curator of Forestry Herbarium (1961–1992) Druce & Fielding Curator (1971–1992) Retired
		David Mabberley Acting Curator (Oxford University Herbaria; 1992–1993) Resigned
		Quentin Cronk Acting Curator (Oxford University Herbaria; 1994) Resigned
		Stephen Harris Druce Curator (Oxford University Herbaria; 1995) Incumbent
Timothy Walker & Alison Foster Co-Directors (January–July 2014) Timothy Walker resigned	Liam Dolan 15th Sherardian Professor (2009) Incumbent	
Alison Foster Acting Director (August 2014–January 2015) Resigned		
Stephen Harris & Charles Shaw Acting Co-Directors (February–June 2015)		
Simon Hiscock Director (July 2015) Incumbent		

* The curator of the herbaria at the Garden and the Department of Botany was the Fielding Curator, the curator of George Druce's British specimens was the Druce Curator and the Department of Forestry herbarium had a separate curator. In 1971 these roles were effectively amalgamated into one post.

Preface

1 All conversions are reported based on the National Archives Currency converter tool (http://www.nationalarchives.gov.uk/currency/) until 2005, with an additional estimation of UK inflation between 2005 and 2015.

2 Garden governance is an essential, if complex and overlooked issue, which has evolved over the Garden's history; irrespective of reporting structures, ultimate responsibility for the Garden lies with the University.

1. Founding the Garden

1 Crossley (1997).
2 Quoted in Chance et al. (1979).
3 Ogilvie (2006).
4 Batey (1986: 31).
5 Chaplin (1920); Allen (1946); Frank (1997).
6 Jones (1956: 273).
7 Worling (2005).
8 Gutch (1796: 335).
9 Daubeny (1853a: 13).
10 McGurk (2004).
11 Hammer (2004).
12 Macnamara (1895: 288–291).
13 Wall (1979).
14 Kelsey (2004).
15 Macnamara (1895: 291–292).
16 Anonymous (1675: 57).
17 Findlen (1994: 256–261).
18 Vines and Druce (1914: x–xii).
19 Page (1907).
20 Vines and Druce (1914: xi).
21 Historic England (2015).
22 Wood (2004); Kelsey (2004).

2. Constructing the Garden

1 Vines and Druce (1914: viii–xiii). The Garden's centenary and bicentenary passed unmarked. Confusion over the Garden's foundation date may explain why the tercentenary was celebrated two years after the foundation date (Druce, 1924). The 350th anniversary was celebrated with the release of a new Guide Book (Darlington and Burras, 1971).

2 Butler (1912: 34).
3 Gibson (1940: 108).
4 The Garden is not aligned along a north–south axis but by tradition the wall parallel to Magdalen College is the North Wall, the wall closest to the river is the East Wall and the wall closest to the city centre is the West Wall.

5 Gunther (1912: 2).
6 Plot (1677: 75).
7 Gutch (1742: 328).
8 Historic England (2015).
9 Hardy and Totelin (2016); Britz (1974).
10 White (2004); Royal Commission on Historical Monuments in England (1939: 14–15).
11 Gunther (1912: Appendix A).
12 Batey (1986: 55).
13 Loggan (1675: plate labelled 'Hortus Botanicus').
14 Mayou and Matthews (2009).
15 Loggan (1675: plate labelled 'Hortus Botanicus'); Williams (1733).
16 Gunther (1912).
17 Loggan (1675) has two engravings that show the Garden; 'Nova & Accuratissima celeberrimae Universitatis Civitatisque Oxoniensis scenographia' and 'Hortus Botanicus'. The former shows the tower which is missing from the latter, Hollar (1643) and all subsequent images of the Garden; Williams (1733).
18 Williams (1733); Oxford Almanack (1766). By 1853, the gates were once again cut by a great circle (Daubeny 1853b: 3).
19 Between the images of the Danby Gate published in Daubeny (1853b: 3) and

Anonymous (1885b: 541) the wooden gate were replaced by the iron gate.

20 Loudon (1838a: 456; Gunther (1912: Appendix A).

21 Anonymous (1675: 56); Gunther (1912: 175).

22 Nineteenth-century images of the Danby Gate show armless statues but a bookplate, apparently from *c.*1790, shows the statues with their limbs intact (Sherardian Library of Plant Taxonomy, Bodleian Library).

3. Planting the Garden

1 Barratt (2015).

2 Crossley (1997: 105–134).

3 Prest (1981); Harvey (1974); Turner (1978).

4 Batey (1986).

5 Vines and Druce (1914: xv).

6 Anonymous (1885a). Figure was drawn by David Loggan and etched by Michael Burghers, men who must have both known Bobart.

7 Allen (2004a); Gunther (1912: 188).

8 Allen (2004a); Anonymous (1885a); Evans (1713: Frontispiece).

9 Bobart (1884).

10 Collection of letters from E. Skwierczynska to Dr Olby, dated March–June 1969 (Sherardian Library of Plant Taxonomy, Bodleian Library).

11 Bobart (1884: 8).

12 Vines and Druce (1914: xvi–xvii).

13 Batey (1986).

14 Sorbière (1709: 42).

15 Magalotti (1821: 262).

16 Gunther (1912: 180).

17 Hearne (1772: 221); Gunther (1912: 180).

18 Mandelbrote (2004).

19 Allen (2004b). Bobart the Elder is buried in the churchyard of St Peters in the East (now part of St Edmund Hall).

20 Various seed lists in Bobart the Younger's hand (British Library; Sloane MS 3343 f.35–36, 45–46, 48, 57, 135–137, 141, 236).

21 Butler (1744: 119).

22 Allen (2004b).

23 Allen (2004c).

24 Smith (1816a).

25 Allen (2004b).

26 Vines and Druce (1914: lv). When Jacob

Bobart the Younger died in 1719, he was buried close to his wife and parents in the churchyard of St Peter's in the East.

27 Gunther (1912: Appendix A).

28 von Uffenbach (1754: 161–162). von Uffenbach's description bears no resemblance to the portrait identified as Bobart the Younger in the Department of Plant Sciences' collection. von Uffenbach also described Bobart's wife as a 'hag'.

29 Anonymous (1648).

30 Stephens and Browne (1658).

31 *Catalogus Herbarum ex horto Botanico Oxoniensis anno collectorum 1676.* Manuscript in Bobart the Younger's hand (MS Sherard 32, Sherardian Library of Plant Taxonomy, Bodleian Library).

32 Three herbarium collections are directly associated with the Bobarts and bear their annotations: the book herbarium of Bobart the Elder, the *Hortus Siccus* of Bobart the Younger and the so-called Morisonian Herbarium associated with the latter Bobart (Oxford University Herbaria); Vines and Druce (1914); Harris (2006).

33 Evans (1713: 29).

34 Pepys (1854: 320).

35 Clokie (1964).

36 Goodman and Walsh (2006).

37 Anonymous (1648: 105); Stephens and Browne (1658: 114); *Catalogus Herbarum ex horto Botanico Oxoniensis anno collectorum 1676.* Manuscript in Bobart the Younger's hand (MS Sherard 32, entry 1175, Sherardian Library of Plant Taxonomy, Bodleian Library); Bobart the Younger's *Hortus Siccus* (BJr-13-084); Bobart the Elder's Herbarium (BSn-M04r-010) (Oxford University Herbaria).

38 Anonymous (1648: 46); Stephens and Browne (1658: 160); Bobart the Elder's Herbarium (BSn-R9r-1) (Oxford University Herbaria).

39 Stephens and Browne (1658: 92); Bobart the Elder's Herbarium (BSn-H12r-6, Oxford University Herbaria).

40 Anonymous (1648: 3); Bobart the Elder's Herbarium (BSn-A09r-07, Oxford University Herbaria).

41 Anonymous (1648); Stephens and Browne (1658).

42 Rea (1665). Named auricula cultivars from

Bobart the Elder Herbarium (BSn-A33r, Oxford University Herbaria).

43 Anonymous (1648: 25); Stephens and Browne (1658: 77); Bobart the Elder's Herbarium (BSn-H05r-5, BSn-H05r-7, Oxford University Herbaria); Griffiths (1888).

44 Label attached to a *Mimosa* specimen in the Morison herbarium (Mor_ii_199_02a_ii, Oxford University Herbaria).

45 Anonymous (1648); Stephens and Browne (1658); *Catalogus Herbarum ex horto Botanico Oxoniensis anno collectorum 1676.* Manuscript in Bobart the Younger's hand (MS Sherard 32, Sherardian Library of Plant Taxonomy, Bodleian Library).

46 Power (1919).

47 Gunther (1912: Appendix A).

48 Anonymous (1648); Stephens and Browne (1658); *Catalogus Herbarum ex horto Botanico Oxoniensis anno collectorum 1676.* Manuscript in Bobart the Younger's hand (MS Sherard 32, Sherardian Library of Plant Taxonomy, Bodleian Library).

4. Evolution

1 John Sibthorp's lecture notes, *c.*1788–1794 (MS Sherard 219, f.19, Sherardian Library of Plant Taxonomy, Bodleian Library).

2 Griffiths (1888).

3 Loggan (1675: plate labelled 'Hortus Botanicus'); Power (1919).

4 Batey (1986); Prest (1981).

5 Hollar (1643); Batey (1986: 52). Hollar's map shows the position of the Garden but it is too small relative to the positions of Magdalen Tower and the Cherwell.

6 Loggan (1675).

7 Batey (1986); Williams' (1733) image of the Garden shows a very formal layout; Addison (1712).

8 Oxford Almanack (1766). The print shows a rather unkempt walled garden with little resemblance to the plan included in the image. The conservatories appear well used and well looked after. The academic in the scene may be Humphrey Sibthorp talking to gardener John Foreman.

9 Sterling (2004).

10 John Sibthorp's lecture notes, *c.*1788–1794

(MS Sherard 219, f.19–20, Sherardian Library of Plant Taxonomy, Bodleian Library).

11 Gunther (1912: 164).

12 Historic England (2015). The superintendent's cottage does not appear on any seventeenth-century maps of the Garden.

13 Linnaeus (1737: Dedicatio).

14 Britz (1974).

15 Thoday (2007).

16 Harris (2011b).

17 John Sibthorp's lecture notes, *c.*1788–1794 (MS Sherard 219, f.380–381, Sherardian Library of Plant Taxonomy, Bodleian Library).

18 Evelyn (1691); Linnaeus (1737: Frontispiece).

19 Britz (1974).

20 Anonymous (1885b: 732).

21 de Beer (2006: entry for 6 August 1685).

22 John Sibthorp's lecture notes, *c.*1788–1794 (MS Sherard 219, f.380, Sherardian Library of Plant Taxonomy, Bodleian Library).

23 Harris (2011b).

24 Letter to Robert Simson, Professor of Mathematics, University of Glasgow from Robert Dick, 14 September 1754 (Corpus of Modern Scottish Writing, http://www.scottishcorpus.ac.uk/cmsw/lifeinoldletters/?documentid=26308&id=P7061122; accessed 14 January 2016).

25 Physic Garden Account 1734 to 1800. (MS Sherard 2, ff.1–20, Sherardian Library of Plant Taxonomy, Bodleian Library)

26 Historic England (2015).

27 Gunther (1912: 179, Appendix A).

28 Manuscript entitled 'Copy of the Decree in Chancery relating to the Physicke Garden to be lodged in ye Library there' (MS Sherard 2, ff. 70v–92v, Sherardian Library of Plant Taxonomy, Bodleian Library).

29 Boulger (2004).

30 Osborn (1943).

5. Revitalization

1 Goddard (2004).

2 Subscriptions to the Botanic Garden Fund. Handwritten accounts by Charles Daubeny. MS Sherard 7, ff.80–81 (Sherardian Library of Plant Taxonomy, Bodleian Library);

Daubeny (1850: 8); Gunther (1912: 24).

3   Report from Charles Daubeny to The Royal
    College of Physicians, dated 14 March 1834
    (MS Sherard 7, f.66); 'Plan of the Botanic
    Garden to be submitted to the Garden
    Committee', annotated by Daubeny. (MS
    Sherard 7, ff.112v–113). (Sherardian Library of
    Plant Taxonomy, Bodleian Library).
4   Hudson (2004).
5   Daubeny (1850: insert map).
6   Daubeny (1853).
7   Matthews (2005).
8   Daubeny (1853b: 20).
9   Daubeny (1850: 30).
10 Holway (2013).
11 Harris (2011b).
12 The charge caused some resentment in 1856
    (Gunther, 1912: 26, 174). Samuel Pepys visit to
    the Garden cost one shilling (£5.70 in 2015)
    on 9 June 1668 (http://www.pepysdiary.
    com/diary/1668/06/; accessed 15 January
    2016).
13 Gunther (1912: 98).
14 Juniper and Dobson (2010).
15 Harris (2015a).
16 Gunther (1912: 98).
17 Gunther (1912: 124).
18 Bower (2004).
19 Gunther (1912: 53); Tuckwell (1908: 35).
20 James (2004).
21 Anonymous (1989: 32).
22 Anonymous (1989: 32).
23 Anonymous (1989: 33).
24 Regulations of the Botanic Garden. Printed
    sheet, dated 29 June 1835. MS Sherard 264,
    f.19v (Sherardian Library of Plant Taxonomy,
    Bodleian Library).
25 Clokie (1964: 5). The relationship between
    Baker and the Garden's governing body and
    users was evidently difficult towards the end
    of his tenure (Sherardian Library of Plant
    Taxonomy, Bodleian Library).
26 Gunther, R.T. (1918) *Second memorandum
    for member of the Hebdomadal Council upon
    the present urgent necessity for economy
    in the management of the Botanic Garden*,
    pp. 13–14. Curators of the Bobart Garden
    (undated) *Further Report of the Curators.
    After considering Mr Gunther's Memorandum.*
    (Sherardian Library of Plant Taxonomy,
    Bodleian Library). Gunther (1934) made a
    forceful case for the importance of retaining
    data and scientific apparatus to understand
    the history of science. The data lost in the
    Garden was fundamental to the scientific
    value of the living plant collections.
27 Harris, S.A., Foster, A., Jones, B. and Price,
    T. 'Debunking a myth: the black pine in
    the Oxford Botanic Garden'. Unpublished
    manuscript.
28 Anonymous (1989: 33).

6. Expansion

1   Schultes (1830). In his Foreword to the
    Schultes (1829), William Hooker tried
    to alleviate some of the author's critical
    overtones by emphasizing his visit was short
    and he was communicating in a foreign
    language.
2   Ogilvie (2006); Endersby (2010).
3   Clokie (1964); Dandy (1958).
4   Daubeny (1850: insert map).
5   Daubeny (1853a). Papers relating to the
    acquisition of the Fielding Herbarium
    (Sherardian Library of Plant Taxonomy,
    Bodleian Library); Jackson (2004).
6   Daubeny (1853a).
7   Harris (2007a).
8   Gunther (1912: 151–152); Mabberley (1995).
9   *Catalogue of the contents of the Botanical
    Museum 1859*, manuscript catalogue
    prepared by William Baxter (MS Sherard
    23, f. 72 f. 79.2–79.4, f.165–170, f.232–235,
    Sherardian Library of Plant Taxonomy,
    Bodleian Library).
10 Notes by Arthur Church (dated 21 April
    1920) inserted into the front of *Catalogue
    of the contents of the Botanical Museum 1859*,
    manuscript catalogue prepared by William
    Baxter (MS Sherard 23, Sherardian Library
    of Plant Taxonomy, Bodleian Library).
11 Daubeny (1841a, 1841b).
12 Goddard (2004).
13 Daubeny (1850: insert map); MS Sherard
    264, ff.15–16 (Sherardian Library of Plant
    Taxonomy, Bodleian Library); Minutes of
    the Governing Body, 25 July 1834, item 5
    (Magdalen College Archive).
14 Daubeny (1850: 23).
15 Daubeny (1853b); Daubeny (1860); Gunther
    (1912: 165–170).

16 Gunther (1912: 165–170).
17 Gunther (1912: 168).
18 Daubeny (1850: 15).
19 Gunther (1912: 49–50).
20 Darlington and Burras (1971: 32).
21 Anonymous (1838); Hartley (2007).
22 Minutes of the Governing Body, 12 October 1843, item 5 (Magdalen College Archive).
23 Daubeny (1853b: 15).
24 Daubeny (1853: 15: insert map, MS Sherard 265a, f.7, Sherardian Library of Plant Taxonomy, Bodleian Library).
25 Minutes of the Governing Body, 9 March 1847, item 2 (Magdalen College Archive); Daubeny (1853: 15: insert map, MS Sherard 265a, f.7, Sherardian Library of Plant Taxonomy, Bodleian Library); Daubeny (1864b: 49).
26 Batey (1979); Piebenga (1994); Handwritten list of stove plants. The folio is undated but inserted into Daubeny's diary between late 1838 and early 1839 (MS Sherard 264, f.47, Sherardian Library of Plant Taxonomy, Bodleian Library).
27 Allen and Walker (1994).

7. Growing Trees

1 Anonymous (1648: 46); Stephens and Browne (1658).
2 Gunther (1912: 35–47).
3 Ma (2003).
4 Gunther (1912: 36–37).
5 Druce (1924).
6 Gunther (1912: 237–244).
7 Anonymous (undated) History of the loss and recovery of Nuneham Courtney Arboretum 1962–1970. Typed manuscript (Sherardian Library of Plant Taxonomy, Bodleian Library).
8 Allen (2006).
9 Batey (1979).
10 Allen and Walker (1994).
11 Batey (1979).
12 Cross (1975).
13 Allen and Walker (1994: 20).
14 Harvey (2002).
15 Allen and Walker (1994: 16).
16 Newth (2008).

8. Engaging People

1 Gunther (1912: Appendix A).
2 Orders for the Physick Garden. Printed sheet, probably mid-eighteenth century. MS Sherard 264, f. 20 (Sherardian Library of Plant Taxonomy, Bodleian Library).
3 Orders for the Physick Garden. Printed sheet, probably early to mid-eighteenth century (MS Sherard 264, f. 20, Sherardian Library of Plant Taxonomy, Bodleian Library).
4 Loggan (1675); Beeverell (1707: 593, 'Jardin de Médecine à Oxford') is a copy of Loggan's print but is populated more visitors and lacks the gardeners.
5 Gunther (1912: 20); Davies (2016).
6 Gunther (1912: Appendix A).
7 Hardy and Totelin (2016: 154–155).
8 Orders for the Physick Garden. Printed sheet, probably mid-eighteenth century. MS Sherard 264, f. 20 (Sherardian Library of Plant Taxonomy, Bodleian Library).
9 Chapman (1883).
10 Regulations of the Botanic Garden. Printed sheet, dated 29 June 1835. MS Sherard 264, f. 19v (Sherardian Library of Plant Taxonomy, Bodleian Library).
11 Daubeny (1850); Daubeny (1853b); Daubeny (1864a); Gunther (1914); Darlington and Robinson (1957); Darlington and Burras (1971) [reprinted 1972, 1980]; Anonymous (1989); Allen and Walker (1994, 1995).
12 Annual Reports relating to the Botanic Garden and to the Department of Botany (Sherardian Library of Plant Taxonomy, Bodleian Library).
13 Gunther (1912: 175).
14 The Gardiner's Oath, 1735 (MS Sherard 1, f.3.r, Sherardian Library of Plant Taxonomy, Bodleian Library).
15 MS Sherard 1, f.19–20 (Sherardian Library of Plant Taxonomy, Bodleian Library).
16 Vines and Druce (1914: xxiv).
17 Clark (1894: 49).
18 Physic Garden Committee Memorandum, dated 7th Feb 1735 (MS Sherard 1, f.5r; Sherardian Library of Plant Taxonomy, Bodleian Library). From the context of the Memorandum, the date is wrong and was corrected at a later date to 7th Feb 1736.
19 Smith (1816b); Clokie (1964: 36).
20 Sibthorp's hand is to be found on specimens,

dated 1750, in the Sherard and Morison herbaria (Oxford University Herbaria).

21 Gascoigne (2004).

22 Document regarding the building of a house and library for the Professor, dated 7 March 1776 (Sherardian Library of Plant Taxonomy, Bodleian Library).

23 Harris (2007b).

24 John Sibthorp's lecture notes, c.1788–1794 (MS Sherard 219, f.20, Sherardian Library of Plant Taxonomy, Bodleian Library).

25 Harris (2011a).

26 John Sibthorp's lecture notes, c.1788–1794 (MS Sherard 219, Sherardian Library of Plant Taxonomy, Bodleian Library).

27 Printed fliers advertising lecture courses by Williams dated 21 April 1819 and 19 April 1817 (Sherardian Library of Plant Taxonomy, Bodleian Library); Tuckwell (1908: 34).

28 Gunther (1904: Appendix E); Tuckwell (1908: 34).

29 Tuckwell, W. (1908: 35).

30 Gunther (1912: 135–136).

31 Phillips (1868).

32 Orders for the Physick Garden. Printed sheet, probably mid-eighteenth century (MS Sherard 264, f. 20, Sherardian Library of Plant Taxonomy, Bodleian Library); Anonymous (1991).

33 John Sibthorp's lecture notes, c.1788–1794 (MS Sherard 219, f.26, Sherardian Library of Plant Taxonomy, Bodleian Library).

34 Hall and Juniper (1981).

35 Anonymous (1885b); Gunther (1912: 29, 123–129, 193). The fate of the specimens at Kew is unknown.

36 Anonymous (2006).

9. Pursuing Science

1 Harris (2015b).

2 Hardy and Totelin (2016).

3 Morton (1981). There is no evidence the Garden had any role in the discovery of plant sexuality, despite Daubeny's (1853: 24) desire for this to be the case; Bennett (1875).

4 Sharrock (1672).

5 Morton (1981).

6 Copy of a Report presented to the Visitors of the Oxford Botanic Garden at their desire by the

Professor of Botany, dated 14 March 1834 (MS Sherard 264, ff.25–26, Sherardian Library of Plant Taxonomy, Bodleian Library).

7 Gunther (1912: 25–26); Copy of a Report presented to the Visitors of the Oxford Botanic Garden at their desire by the Professor of Botany, dated 14 March 1834 (MS Sherard 264, ff.25–26, Sherardian Library of Plant Taxonomy, Bodleian Library). In the early nineteenth century, 'Botanical Garden' was used in lecture fliers (Printed fliers dated 21 April 1819 and 19 April 1817, Sherardian Library of Plant Taxonomy, Bodleian Library). During the 1970s, the Garden was known as the 'Botanic Gardens' through the incorporation of the 'Genetic Garden' and the 'Arboretum' (Darlington and Burras, 1971).

8 Darlington (1954); Darlington and Burras (1971: 3, 6).

9 Mandelbrote (2015).

10 Vines and Druce (1914: xxvi–xxvii); Mandelbrote (2015).

11 Raven (1950).

12 Druce and Vines (1907).

13 Blunt (2004: 112–114).

14 Calmann (1977: 80–81); MS Sherard 1, f.19–20 (Sherardian Library of Plant Taxonomy, Bodleian Library).

15 Harris (2008).

16 Harris (2007b).

17 John Sibthorp's lecture notes, c.1788–1794 (MS Sherard 219, f.19, Sherardian Library of Plant Taxonomy, Bodleian Library); Harris (2007b).

18 Allen (2016).

19 Harris (2011b).

20 Letter from Jacob Bobart the Younger to Mary Somerset, Duchess of Badminton, dated 28 March 1694 [British Library; Sloane MS 3343 ff.37r–37v].

21 'Mr Bobarts' Catalogue of Plants att Oxon. Plants that may be had of Mr Bobart 1693'. Manuscript in Bobart the Younger's hand [British Library; Sloane MS 3343 f.19]; Ogilvie (2006).

22 Sharrock (1672: 116).

23 Sharrock (1672: 69–70).

24 Sharrock (1672: 116); Plot (1677: 260).

25 Batey (1986: 41).

26 Gunther (1912: 165–167); Gunther (1904).

27 Anonymous (1648); Stephens and Browne (1658).

28 Miller (1768: RUB).
29 Morison (1669: 194).
30 Plot (1677: 172); Stephens and Browne (1658: 104); *Catalogus Herbarum ex horto Botanico Oxoniensis anno collectorum 1676*. Manuscript in Bobart the Younger's hand (MS Sherard 32, entries 231.2, 483 & 1061, Sherardian Library of Plant Taxonomy, Bodleian Library); Bobart the Elder's Herbarium (BSn-A03r-09, Oxford University Herbaria).
31 Burras (1974); Woudstra (2006).
32 Harris (2007b).
33 Gunther (1912: 30).
34 Ward (1852); Allen (1984).
35 Gunther (1912: 131).
36 Prest (1981).
37 Miller, P. (1768: GEN); Blair (1720: 272).
38 Jacob Bobart's list of woody plants in his own hand (MS Sherard 34, f.30v, entry 0476, 'Platanus inter Orientalem et Occidentalem media', Sherardian Library of Plant Taxonomy, Bodleian Library); specimen appears to be missing from the herbarium.
39 Harris (2002).
40 Allan and Pannell (2009).
41 Harris (2002).
42 Dandy (1958: 92).
43 Gunther (1912: 26).

10. Splitting Apart

1   Daubeny (1853a: 13).
2   Gunther (1912: 28).
3   Internal papers for the University Council by Marmaduke Lawson dated 20 November 1875 and 14 February 1876 (Sherardian Library of Plant Taxonomy, Bodleian Library).
4   Gunther (1912: 28).
5   Gunther (1912).
6   Eighteenth-century and nineteenth-century account books of the Garden (MS Sherard 2 to Ms Sherard 4); report from Charles Daubeny to the Board of Heads of Houses and Proctors pleading of an increased allowance for Garden maintenance, dated 30 January 1840 (MS Sherard 7, ff.121–127) (Sherardian Library of Plant Taxonomy, Bodleian Library).
7   Gunther (1916).
8   Anonymous (1951).
9   Smith and Marks (c.1961: 11).
10 Walker (2013).
11 Foster (2014).
12 Price (2013).
13 Walker (2005).
14 Foster (c.2010).

Addison, J. (1712) *Spectator* 414: 499–500.

Allan, E. and Pannell, J. R. (2009) 'Rapid Divergence in Physiological and Life-History Traits between Northern and Southern Populations of the British Introduced Neo-species', *Senecio squalidus*. Oikos 118: 1053–1061.

Allen, D. E. (1984) *The Naturalist in Britain: A Social History*. Princeton, NJ: Princeton University Press.

Allen, D. E. (2004a) 'Bobart, Jacob, the Elder (*c.*1599–1680)', *Oxford Dictionary of National Biography*, Oxford University Press [http://www.oxforddnb.com/view/article/2741, accessed 14 December 2015].

Allen, D. E. (2004b) 'Bobart, Jacob, the Younger (1641–1719)', *Oxford Dictionary of National Biography*. Oxford University Press [http://ezproxy-prd.bodleian.ox.ac.uk:2167/view/article/2742, accessed 24 December 2015].

Allen, D. E. (2004c) 'Sherard, William (1659–1728)', *Oxford Dictionary of National Biography*, Oxford University Press [http://www.oxforddnb.com/view/article/25355, accessed 1 February 2016].

Allen, L. (2006) 'The Final Word', *Botanic Garden News* 63: 12.

Allen, L. and Walker, T. (1994) *The Harcourt Arboretum, Nuneham Courtenay, Oxfordshire.* Oxford: The University of Oxford Botanic Garden.

Allen, L. and Walker, T. (1995) *The University of Oxford Botanic Garden*. Oxford: University of Oxford Botanic Garden.

Allen, M. (2016) 'The Oxford University Botanic Garden and Harcourt Arboretum Florilegium Society (and a short history of botanical illustration)'. *Botanic Garden & Harcourt Arboretum Friends Newsletter* 92: 7–8.

Allen, P. (1946) 'Medical Education in 17th century England'. *Journal of the History of Medicine and Allied Sciences* 1: 115–143.

Anonymous (1648) *Catalogus Plantarum Horti Medici Oxoniensis*. Oxonii: Henricus Hall.

Anonymous (1675) *Mock Songs and Joking Poems, All Novel; Consisting of Mocks to Several Late Songs about the Town*. London: printed for William Birtch.

Anonymous (1838) 'A Tabular View of the Species of Abiétinae Contained in the Principal Pinetums and Collections of Abiétinae in Great Britain, and on the Continent of Europe'. *Gardener's Magazine* 14: 29–32.

Anonymous (1885a) 'Jacob Bobart'. *Gardeners' Chronicle* 24: 208–209.

Anonymous (1885b) 'The Oxford Botanic Garden'. *Gardeners' Chronicle* 23: 540–541, 732–733.

Anonymous (1951) *University of Oxford. Department of Botany. Opening of the New Building by the Lord Rothschild*. Oxford: Oxford University Press.

Anonymous (1989) *The University of Oxford Botanic Garden*. Oxford: The University of Oxford Botanic Garden.

Anonymous (1991) 'Editorial'. *News. University of Oxford Botanic Garden*. 1: 2.

Anonymous (2006) 'A look at Recent Developments at the Garden and Arboretum'. *Botanic Garden News* 63: 5.

Barratt, J. (2015) *Cavalier Capital. Oxford in the English Civil War 1642–1646*. Solihull: Helion & Company Limited.

Batey, M. (1986) *Oxford Gardens. The University's Influence on Garden History*. Aldershot: Scolar Press.

Batey, M.L. (1979) *Nuneham Courtenay Oxfordshire. A Short History and Description of the House, Gardens, and Estate.* Oxford: University of Oxford.

Beeverell, J. (1707) *Les délices de la Grand' Bretagne et de l'Irlande,* vol. 3. Leiden: Pierre Vander Aa.

Bennett, A.W. (1875) 'Sir Thomas Millington and the Sexuality of Plants'. *Nature* 13: 85–86.

Blair, P. (1720) *Botanisk Essays.* London: printed by Williams and John Innys.

Blunt, W. (2004) *Linnaeus. The Compleat Naturalist.* London: Frances Lincoln.

Bobart, H.T. (1884) *A Biographical Sketch of Jacob Bobart, of Oxford, Together with an Account of his Two Sons, Jacob and Tilleman.* Leicester: printed for private circulation only.

Boulger, G.S. (2004) 'Dillenius, Johann Jakob (1687–1747)', *Oxford Dictionary of National Biography* [http://www.oxforddnb.com/view/article/7648, accessed 1 February 2016].

Bower, F.O. (2004) Balfour, Sir Isaac Bayley (1853–1922). *Oxford Dictionary of National Biography* [http://www.oxforddnb.com/view/article/30558, accessed 1 February 2016].

Bradley, R. (1718) *New Improvements of Planting and Gardening, both Philosophical and Practical; Explaining the Motion of the Sapp and Generation of Plants.* London: W. Mears.

Britz, B.S. (1974) 'Environmental Provisions for Plants in Seventeenth-Century Northern Europe'. *The Journal of the Society of Architectural Historians* 33: 133–144.

Burras, J.K. (1974) 'The Nature of Variegation'. *Journal of the Royal Horticultural Society* 99: 440–443.

Butler, C.V. (1912) *Social Conditions in Oxford.* London: Sidgwick & Jackson Ltd.

Butler, S. (1744) *Hudibras, in Three Parts, Written in the Time of the Late Wars: Corrected and Amended. with Large Annotations, and a Preface, by Zachary Grey,* vol. 1. Dublin: Printed for Robert Owen and William Brien.

Calmann, G. (1977) *Ehret. Flower Painter Extraordinary.* Oxford: Phaidon.

Chance, E., Colvin, C., Cooper, J., Day, C.J., Hassall, T.G., Jessup, M. and Selwyn, N. (1979) 'Early Modern Oxford', in A. Crossley and C.R. Elrington (eds), *A History of the County of Oxford: Volume 4, the City of Oxford.* Oxford: Oxford University Press, pp. 74–180.

Chaplin, A. (1920) 'The History of Medical Education in the Universities of Oxford and Cambridge, 1500–1850'. *Proceedings of the Royal Society of Medicine* 13: 83–107.

Chapman, E. (1883) *Report of the Botanic Garden for 1883.* Oxford: Oxford Botanic Garden.

Clark, A. (1894) *The Life and Times of Anthony Wood, Antiquary, of Oxford, 1632–1695,* vol. e: *1682–1695.* Oxford: printed for the Oxford Historical Society, at the Clarendon Press.

Clokie H.N. (1964) *An Account of the Herbaria of the Department of Botany in the University of Oxford.* Oxford: Oxford University Press.

Cross, J.R. (1975) *Rhododendron Ponticum* L. *Journal of Ecology* 63: 345–364.

Crossley, A. (1997) 'City and University', in N. Tyacke, *The History of the University of Oxford,* vol. 4: *Seventeenth-Century Oxford.* Oxford: Clarendon, pp. 105–134.

Dandy, J.E. (1958) *The Sloane Herbarium: An Annotated List of the Horti Sicci Composing it with Biographical Accounts of the Principal Contributors, Based on Records Compiled by the Late James Britten.* London: printed by order of the Trustees of the British Museum.

Darlington, C.D. (1954) *The Place of Botany in the Life of a University. An Inaugural Lecture Delivered before the University of Oxford on 27 November 1953.* Oxford: the Clarendon Press.

Darlington, C.D. (1971) 'The Oxford Botanic Gardens: 1621 to 1971'. *Nature* 233: 455–456.

Darlington, C.D. and Burras, J.K. (1971) *Guide to the Oxford Botanic Gardens.* Oxford: privately published.

Darlington, C.D. and Robinson, G.W. (1957) *Oxford Botanic Garden Guide*. Oxford: Basil Blackwell.

Daubeny, C. (1841a) *Three Lectures in Agriculture; Delivered at Oxford, on July 22nd, and Nov. 25th, 1840, and on Jan. 26th, 1841, in which Chemical Operation of Manures is Particularly Considered, and the Scientific Principles Explained, upon which their Efficacy Appears to Depend*. Oxford: John Murray.

Daubeny, C. (1841b) 'Editorial'. *The Gardeners' Chronicle* 1841: 1.

Daubeny, C. (1850) *Oxford Botanic Garden, or, a Popular Guide to the Botanic Garden of Oxford*. Oxford: printed by I. Shrimpton.

Daubeny, C. (1853a) *Address to the Members of the University. Delivered on May 20, 1853*. Oxford: Botanic Garden.

Daubeny, C. (1853b) *Oxford Botanic Garden; or a Popular Guide to the Botanic Garden of Oxford*. 2nd edition. Oxford: printed by Messrs. Parker.

Daubeny, C. (1860) 'The Oxford Experimental Garden'. *Gardeners' Chronicle* 1860: 630–631.

Daubeny, C. (1864a) *Oxford Botanic Garden; or a Popular Guide to the Botanic Garden of Oxford*. 2nd edition with supplement. Sold at the Botanic Garden only, Oxford [overprinted 'Corrected to 1866'].

Daubeny, C. (1864b) *Supplement to the Botanic Garden Guide*. Oxford: printed by Messrs. Parker.

Davies, M. (2016) *King of All Balloons: The Adventurous Life of James Sadler, the First English Aeronaut*. Chalford: Amberley Publishing.

de Beer, E.S. (2006) *The Diary of John Evelyn*. London: Everyman's Library.

Druce, G.C. (1924) 'Oxford Botanic Garden – Foundation and Tercentenary'. *Report of the Botanical Exchange Club* 1923: 335–366.

Druce, G.C. and Vines, S.H. (1907) *The Dillenian Herbaria. An Account of the Dillenian Collections in the Herbarium of the University of Oxford*. Oxford: Clarendon Press.

Endersby, J. (2010) *Imperial Nature: Joseph Hooker and the Practices of Victorian Science*. Chicago: The University of Chicago Press

Evans, A. (1713) *Vertumnus. An Epistle to Mr. Jacob Bobart, Botany Professor to the University of Oxford, and Keeper of the Physick Garden*. Oxford: printed by L.L. for Stephen Fletcher Bookseller.

Evelyn, J. (1691) *Kalendarium Hortense: or, the Gard'ners Almanac,: Directing What He is to Do Monthly throughout the Year. and What Fruits and Flowers are in Prime*. London, R. Chiswell in St. Paul's Church-yard, T. Sawbridge in Little-Britain, and R. Bently in Russel-street in Covent-garden.

Findlen P. (1994) *Possessing Nature. Museums, Collecting, and Scientific Culture in Early Modern Italy*. Berkeley: University of California Press.

Foster, A. (c.2010) *The Medicinal Plant Collection at the University of Oxford Botanic Garden*. Oxford: University of Oxford Botanic Garden.

Foster, A. (2014) 'Oxford Plants 400. *Heliamphora nutans* Benth. (Sarraceniaceae)'. *Oxford Plant Systematics* 20: 15.

Frank, R.G. (1997) 'Medicine', in N. Tyacke, *The History of the University of Oxford. Vol. 4, Seventeenth-Century Oxford*. Oxford: Clarendon, pp. 505–557.

Gascoigne, J. (2004) 'Banks, Sir Joseph, Baronet (1743–1820)'. *Oxford Dictionary of National Biography*, Oxford University Press; online edn, September 2013 [http://www.oxforddnb.com/view/article/1300, accessed 19 January 2016].

Gibson, S. (1940) 'Brian Twyne'. *Oxoniensia* 5: 94–114.

Goddard, N. (2004) 'Daubeny, Charles Giles Bridle (1795–1867)'. *Oxford Dictionary of National Biography* [http://www.oxforddnb.com/view/article/7187, accessed 1 February 2016].

Goodman, J. and Walsh, V. (2006) *The Story of Taxol: Nature and Politics in the Pursuit of an Anti-Cancer Drug*. Cambridge: Cambridge University Press.

Griffiths, E.W. (1888) *Through England on a Side Saddle in the Time of William and Mary Being the Diary of Celia Fiennes.* London: Field & Tuer, The Leadenhall Press, E.C. Simpkin, Marshall & Co.; Hamilton, Adams & Co.

Gunther, R.T. (1904) *A History of the Daubeny Laboratory, Magdalen College, Oxford: to which is Appended a List of the Writings of Dr. Daubeny, and a Register of the Names of Persons Who Have Attended the Chemical Lectures of Dr. Daubeny from 1822 to 1867.* London: Henry Frowde, Oxford University Press.

Gunther, R.T. (1912) *Oxford Gardens Based upon Daubeny's Popular Guide of the Physick Garden of Oxford: with Notes on the Gardens of the Colleges and on the University Park.* Oxford: Parker & Son.

Gunther, R.T. (1914) *A Guide to the Oxford Botanic Garden: with Notes on Recent Additions.* Oxford: University of Oxford Botanic Garden.

Gunther, R.T. (1916) *The Daubeny Laboratory Register 1904–1915: with Notes on the Teaching of Natural Philosophy and with Lists of Scientific Researches Carried Out by Members of Magdalen College, Oxford.* Oxford, printed for the subscribers at the University Press.

Gunther, R.T. (1934) *Oxford and the History of Science. Inaugural Lecture Delivered in the Examination Schools 25 October 1934.* London: Oxford University Press.

Gutch, J. (1742) *The History and Antiquities of the University of Oxford in Two Books: by Anthony à Wood,* vol. 1. Oxford: printed for the Editor.

Gutch, J. (1796) *The History and Antiquities of the University of Oxford in Two Books: by Anthony à Wood, M.A. of Merton College,* vol. 2. Oxford: printed for the Editor.

Hall, T.H.R. and Juniper, B.E. (1981) 'Pottery Plant Labels'. *Country Life* 24 September, p. 1022.

Hammer, P.E.J. (2004) 'Danvers, Sir Charles (c.1568–1601)'. *Oxford Dictionary of National Biography.* Oxford University Press; online edn, January 2008 [http://www.oxforddnb.com/view/article/7132, accessed 3 December 2015].

Hardy, G. and Totelin, L. (2016) *Ancient Botany.* London: Routledge.

Harris, S.A. (2002) 'Introduction of Oxford Ragwort, *Senecio squalidus* L. (Asteraceae), to the United Kingdom'. *Watsonia* 24: 31–43.

Harris, S.A. (2006) 'Bobart the Younger's *Hortus Siccus*'. *Oxford Plant Systematics* 13: 10–11.

Harris, S.A. (2007a) 'Druce and the Oxford University Herbaria'. *Oxford Plant Systematics* 14: 12–13.

Harris, S.A. (2007b) *The Magnificent* Flora Graeca. *How the Mediterranean Came to the English Garden.* Oxford: Bodleian Library.

Harris, S.A. (2008) 'Sibthorp, Bauer and the *Flora Graeca*'. *Oxford Plant Systematics* 15: 7–8.

Harris, S.A. (2011a) 'John Sibthorp: a Teacher of Botany'. *Oxford Plant Systematics* 17: 16–17.

Harris, S.A. (2011b) *Planting Paradise: Cultivating the Garden 1501–1900.* Oxford: Bodleian Library.

Harris, S.A. (2015a) 'The Plant Collections of Mark Catesby in Oxford', in E.C. Nelson and D.J. Elliott (eds), *The Curious Mister Catesby.* Athens: The University of Georgia Press.

Harris, S.A. (2015b) *What Have Plants Ever Done for Us? Western Civilization in Fifty Plants.* Oxford: Bodleian Library.

Hartley, B. (2007) 'Sites of Knowledge and Instruction: Arboretums and the "Arboretum et Fruticetum Britannicum"'. *Garden History* 35: 28–52.

Harvey, G. (2002) *The Forgiveness of Nature. The Story of Grass.* London: Vintage.

Harvey, J. (1974) *Early Nurserymen.* London: Phillimore.

Hearne, T. (1772) *The Life of Anthony à Wood from the Year 1632 to 1672.* Eton: printed for J. and J. Fletcher in the Turl; and J. Pote.

Historic England (2015) Listing. Oxford Botanic Garden. [https://historicengland.org.uk/listing/the-list/list-entry/1000464 accessed 15 January 2016].

Hollar, W. (1643) Oxforde. 1:6,000 map. London: F. Constable.

Holway, T. (2013) *The Flower of Empire: An Amazonian Water Lily, the Quest to Make it Bloom, and the World it Created*. Oxford: Oxford University Press.

Hudson, G. (2004) 'Baxter, William (1787–1871)'. *Oxford Dictionary of National Biography*. [http://www.oxforddnb.com/view/article/1740, accessed 1 February 2016].

Jackson, B.D. (2004) 'Fielding, Henry Borron (1805–1851)'. *Oxford Dictionary of National Biography* [http://www.oxforddnb.com/view/article/9401, accessed 1 February 2016].

James, W.O. (2004) 'Keeble, Sir Frederick William (1870–1952)'. *Oxford Dictionary of National Biography* [http://www.oxforddnb.com/view/article/34254, accessed 1 February 2016].

Jones, W.H.S. (1956) *Pliny. Natural History. Books XXIV–XXVII*. London: Harvard University Press.

Juniper, B.E. and Dobson, M. (2010) 'A Malignant Fever Might Result'. *Oxford Magazine* 302: 15–16.

Kelsey, S. (2004) 'Danvers, Sir John (1584/5–1655)'. *Oxford Dictionary of National Biography*. Oxford University Press; online edn, January 2009 [http://www.oxforddnb.com/view/article/7135, accessed 4 December 2015].

Linnaeus, C. (1737) *Hortus Cliffortianus, plantas exhibens quas. Hartecampi coluit Georgius Clifford*. Amstelaedami.

Loggan, D. (1675) *Oxonia illustrata, sive, omnium celeberrimae istius universitatis collegiorum, aularum, bibliothecae Bodleianae, scholarum publicarum, Theatri Sheldoniani, nec non urbis totius scenographia*. e Theatro Sheldoniano, Oxoniae.

Loudon, J.C. (1838a) *An Encyclopaedia of Gardening*. London: Longman, Hurst, Rees, Orme, Brown, and Green.

Loudon, J.C. (1838b) *Arboretum et Fruticetum Britannicum; or, The Trees and Shrubs of Britain*, vol. 1. London: Printed for the author, p. 2.

Ma, J. (2003) 'The Chronology of the "Living Fossil" *Metasequoia glyptostroboides* (Taxodiaceae): a Review (1943–2003)'. *Harvard Papers in Botany* 8: 9–18.

Mabberley, D. (1995) 'The Oxford Botanical Museum and its Fate'. *Oxford Plant Systematics* 3: 15–16.

Macnamara, F.N. (1895) *Memorials of the Danvers Family (of Dauntsey and Culworth)*. London: Hardy & Page.

Magalotti, L. (1821) *Travels of Cosmo the Third, Grand Duke of Tuscany, through England, During the Reign of King Charles the Second (1669)*. London: J. Mawman.

Mandelbrote, S. (2004) 'Morison, Robert (1620–1683)'. *Oxford Dictionary of National Biography*. Oxford University Press, Oxford. [http://ezproxy-prd.bodleian.ox.ac.uk:2167/view/article/19275, accessed 24 December 2015].

Mandelbrote, S. (2015) 'The Publication and Illustration of Robert Morison's *Plantarum historiae universalis Oxoniensis*'. *Huntington Library Quarterly* 78: 349–379.

Matthews, J. (2005) 'Four Nineteenth-Century Garden Ornaments in the Oxford Botanic Garden'. *Garden History* 33: 274–285.

Mayou, R. and Matthews, J. (2009) 'The Garden Buildings'. *Botanic Garden News* 73: 4–7.

McGurk, J.J.N. (2004) 'Danvers, Henry, earl of Danby (1573–1644)'. *Oxford Dictionary of National Biography*. Oxford University Press; online edn, May 2009 [http://www.oxforddnb.com/view/article/7133, accessed 3 December 2015]

Miller, P. (1768) *The Gardeners Dictionary: Containing the Best and Newest Methods pf Cultivating and Improving the Kitchen, Fruit, Flower Garden and Nursery*. Printed for the Author, London.

Morison, R. (1669) *Hortus Regius Blesensis auctus*. Tho. Roycroft, Londoni.

Morton, A.G. (1981) *History of Botanical Science: An Account of the Development of Botany from Ancient Times to the Present Day*. London: Academic Press.

Newth, P. (2008) 'Creating the Palmer's Leys Meadow'. *Botanic Garden News* 70: 6–7.

Ogilvie, B.W. (2006) *The Science of Describing: Natural History in Renaissance Europe*. Chicago: University of Chicago Press.

Osborn, T.G.B. (1943) 'Changes at the Botanic Gardens'. *The Oxford Magazine*, 11 March.

Oxford Almanack (1766). Print etched by Samuel Wale.

Page, W. (1907) 'Hospitals: St John the Baptist, Oxford', in A. Crossley and C.R. Elrington (eds), *A History of the County of Oxford*, vol. 4: *The City of Oxford*. London: Victoria County History, pp. 158–159.

Pepys, S. (1854) *Diary and Correspondence of Samuel Pepys, F.R.S., the Diary Deciphered by J. Smith, with a Life and Notes by Richard Lord Braybrooke*, vol. 2. London: Henry Colburn.

Phillips, J. (1868) 'Obituary notice of Charles Giles Brindle Daubeny, M.D., F.R.S., sometime Professor of Chemistry, and late Professor of Botany and of Rural Economy in the University of Oxford'. *Proceedings of the Ashmolean Society* 5: 1–15.

Piebenga, S. (1994) 'William Sawrey Gilpin (1762–1843): Picturesque Improver'. *Garden History* 22: 175–196.

Plot, R. (1677) *The Natural History of Oxford-shire, Being an Essay toward the Natural History of England*. Oxford: printed at the Theater.

Power, D. (1919) 'The Oxford Physic Garden'. *Annals of Medical History* 2: 109–125.

Prest, J. (1981) *The Garden of Eden. The Botanic Garden and the Re-creation of Paradise*. New Haven, CT, and London: Yale University Press.

Price, T. (2013) 'Plant Conservation on Our Doorstep – Helping Prevent Local Plant Extinctions'. *Botanic Garden and Harcourt Arboretum News* 85: 8–9.

Raven, C.E. (1950) *John Ray: Naturalist*. Cambridge: Cambridge University Press.

Rea, J. (1665) *Flora, seu, de florum cultura, or, a Complete florilege: Furnished with all the Requisites Belonging to a Florists. In III Books*. London: printed by J.G. for Thomas Clarke.

Royal Commission on Historical Monuments in England (1939) *An Inventory of the Historical Monuments in the City of Oxford*. London: His Majesty's Stationery Office.

Schultes, J.A. (1829) 'On the Cultivation of Botany in England'. *The Philosophical Magazine* 6: 351–366.

Schultes, J.A. (1830) 'Schultes's Botanical Visit to England'. *Botanical Miscellany* 1: 48–78.

Sharrock, R. (1672) *The History of the Propagation & Improvement of Vegetables by the Concurrence of Art and Nature*. Oxford: printed by W. Hall, for Ric. Davis.

Smith, D. and Marks, G. (c.1961) *New Oxford. A Guide to the Modern City*. Oxford: Oxford University Design Society.

Smith, J.E. (1816a) 'Sherard, William', in A. Rees (ed.), *The New Cyclopaedia*, vol. 32, part 2. London: Longman, Hurst, Rees, Orme, and Brown.

Smith, J.E. (1816b) 'Sibthorpia', in A. Rees (ed.), *The New Cyclopaedia*, vol. 32, part 2. London: Longman, Hurst, Rees, Orme, and Brown.

Sorbière, S. (1709) *A Voyage to England: Containing Many Things Relating to the State of Learning, Religion, and other Curiosities of that Kingdom. As also, Observations on the Same Voyage, by Dr. Thomas Sprat, Lord Bishop of Rochester. With a Letter of Monsieur Sorbière's, Concerning the War between England and Holland in 1652: to all which is Prefix'd his Life Writ by M. Graverol*. London: J. Woodward.

Stephens, J. (1966) 'Wood Extension to Botanic Garden'. *The Times*, 6 December.

Stephens, P. and Browne, W. (1658) *Catalogus Horti Botanici Oxoniensis*. Oxonii, Typis Gulielmi Hall.

Sterling, K.B. (2004) 'Sibthorp, John (1758–1796)'. *Oxford Dictionary of National Biography* [http://www.oxforddnb.com/view/article/25509, accessed 1 February 2016].

Thoday P. (2007) *Two Blades of Grass. The Story of Cultivation*. Corsham: Thoday Associates.

Tuckwell, W. (1908) *Reminiscences of Oxford*. New York: E.P. Button & Company.

Turner, J. (1978) 'Ralph Austen, an Oxford Horticulturist of the Seventeenth Century'. *Garden History* 6: 39–45.

Vines, S.H. and Druce, G.C. (1914) *An Account of the Morisonian Herbarium in the Possession of the University of Oxford*. Oxford: Clarendon Press.

von Uffenbach, Z.C. (1754) *Merkwürdige Reisen durch Niedersachsen, Holland und Engelland, Dritter Theil*. Ulm: auf Rosten der Baumischen Handlung.

Walker, T. (2005) 'Classification and Phylogeny at the Oxford Botanic Garden'. *Oxford Plant Systematics* 12: 10.

Walker, T. (2013) *Plant Conservation. Why it Matters and How it Works*. Portland, OR: Timber Press.

Wall, A. (1979) 'The Feud and Shakespeare's *Romeo and Juliet*: a Reconsideration'. *Sydney Studies in English* 5: 84–95.

Ward, N.B. (1852) *On the Growth of Plants in Closely Glazed Cases*. London: John von Voorst.

White, A. (2004) 'Stone, Nicholas (1585?–1647)'. *Oxford Dictionary of National Biography*. Oxford University Press, [http://www.oxforddnb.com/view/article/26577, accessed 8 December 2015].

Williams, W. (1733) *Oxonia depicta sive Collegiorum et aularum in inclyta Academia Oxoniensi ichnographica, orthographica & scenographica delineati: LXV tabulis aeneis*. Oxford: William Williams.

Wood, J. (2004) 'Dyck, Sir Anthony Van (1599–1641)'. *Oxford Dictionary of National Biography*. Oxford University Press; online edn, May 2010 [http://www.oxforddnb.com/view/article/28081, accessed 3 December 2015].

Worling, P.M. (2005) 'Pharmacy in the Early Modern World, 1617 to 1841 AD', in S. Anderson (ed.), *Making Medicines. A Brief History of Pharmacy and Pharmaceuticals*. London: Pharmaceutical Press, pp. 57–76.

Woudstra, J. (2006) '"Striped Plants": The First Collections of Variegated Plants in Late Seventeenth-century Gardens'. *Garden History* 34: 64–79.

PICTURE CREDITS

INDEX

INDEX